American English

Business Phrasal Verbs
and collocations

Stephanie Burdine and Michael Barlow

ISBN: 978-0-940753-19-8

Illustrations by Hurst Vanrooj

Athelstan
5925 Kirby Drive
Suite E 464
Houston TX 77005
USA

www.athel.com
www.corpuslab.com
info@athel.com

To the Student

The CorpusLAB series of books are based on computer-aided analysis of spoken and written American English. By studying the exercises in this book, you will be learning the most frequent phrasal verbs and associated phrases (collocations) in Business English and you will be working with the spoken and written sentences you are likely to encounter in business situations.

All the phrasal verbs in this book are very frequent in English.

Meaning. We give several common meanings for each phrasal verb. These meanings are often extensions from the core meaning and they may be abstract. You should study the sentences carefully to see how each phrasal verb is used.

Collocations. Each meaning of a phrasal verb is usually associated with a set of particular words (collocates) within the sentence. For example, *complaints* is a frequent collocate of *deal with*, as in the sentence *we had to deal with a lot of complaints*. When you work through the units in *Business Phrasal Verbs*, you will not only learn common phrasal verbs, you will also learn longer phrases such as *deal with complaints*.

Idioms. Phrasal verbs are often used in idioms, such as the expression *look at the big picture*. We have included the more frequent idioms in this book

Each unit concentrates on one phrasal verb (e.g., *go out*). The phrasal verb is introduced in a table format that (a) highlights the grammar of the phrasal verb, (b) defines its most common meanings, and (c) provides examples of how the phrasal verb is used in business English. The information in the table is brief, easy-to-follow, and can be consulted at any time for quick reference.

Each table is followed by a series of exercises intended to check your understanding of the meaning and uses of the phrasal verb presented in the unit. The exercises generally progress from controlled practice to more open-ended exercises. A wide variety of question types are used; including, fill-in-the-blanks, multiple choice, sentence matching, and re-writing, as well as pattern identification, error correction, and discussion.

Following every four units, you will find a short set of comprehensive review exercises to consolidate your learning of the phrasal verbs in the previous four chapters. There are also six CorpusLAB units which provide more corpus data and provide opportunities for developing a deeper understanding of the material through a technique called data-driven learning in which you will analyze and classify phrasal verb usage.

You will also find a key to all of the exercises at the end of the book, which you can use to check your answers. The index contains a list of a list of the phrasal verbs and collocations used in the book.

*I need to **draw up** a plan*

*We're ready to **roll out** our new product*

CONTENTS

Unit 1: DEAL WITH someone/something

STUDY THESE SENTENCES

The management failed to **deal with** widespread problems within the company.
I told him I deal with all foreign sales.
I'd rather deal with you guys
We'll continue to **deal with** the Russian government.
The guidelines **deal with** topics such as sales and marketing.
Her newspaper articles often **dealt with** problems at work.

1   handle

2   do business with

3   cover, be concerned with

EXERCISES

A. Using the information above, decide which use of *deal with* is illustrated in each of the following examples. Write the number on the line:

1. We'd prefer to deal with a single supplier.   _____
2. Her advice column usually deals with interoffice problems and how to solve them.   _____
3. The company will have to deal with several contaminated sites.   _____

B. Rewrite the sentences by replacing the underlined word or phrase with the correct form of *deal with* (e.g. *is dealing with*).

1. The bank <u>services</u> a number of US corporations.

2. He likes his job and <u>meeting</u> people.

3. In my field of work, you <u>handle</u> a wide variety of issues.

4. Some companies only <u>offer services to</u> very wealthy people.

5. The translators have <u>processed</u> thousands of pages of documents.

C. Complete the sentences with a suitable form of *deal with* (e.g., *is dealing with*) and one of the words from the box. Be sure to use the correct article (e.g. *a*/*the*) with the noun where required:

lawsuit	manufacturers	companies	corruption	sales

1. We plan to .... in China.

2. There was a recognition that .... is a problem and that it has to be .... :

3. The lawyer said we may have to ...."

4. The company has to find ways to .... the drop in ...."

5. All .... now have to .... environmental concerns.

I think you may have to deal with some complaints here

UNIT 2: LOOK AT someone/something

STUDY THESE SENTENCES

He **looked at** me for a few seconds.   1   **Basic meaning**
*Just **look at** those million-dollar houses!*   = turn eyes toward
We are **looking at** improving our packaging.   2   **Extended meaning**
                                                                                       examine, study, consider
We'll **look at** the possibility of a merger.

IDIOMS
*Ryan, let's **look at the big picture**.*   3   **look at the big picture**
                                                                                       = consider the whole situation

EXERCISES

A. Create full sentences using the words provided in the brackets and an appropriate
      form of *look at*. Include articles (*the/a*) with nouns where required. The first one has
      been done for you.

   1. (accountant/sales figures/for July) The accountant looked at sales figures for
       July.
   2. (He/often/his computer/to check for new email) ....
       ....:
   3. (She/recommends/utility stocks) ....
   4. (We're/a variety of ways/to cut costs) ....
   5. (I/always/problem/and/try to solve it/step by step) ....
       ....:

B. Match the beginning of each sentence with the most appropriate ending:

   1. The audit looked at   the big picture.
   2. The panel will look at   It reinvented its entire economy.
   3. The report looked at   loans made in 2002.
   4. Look at Asia today.   both sides of the tax issue.
   5. The important thing for her is to look at   smoking trends among teenagers.

C. Correct the errors in these sentences. There is one error in each sentence:

   1. I don't know if you've had a chance to looked at the book yet.
   2. We looked on some potential acquisitions in the UK.
   3. Most people looks at it as an investment.
   4. The study look at the top 100 companies.
   5. If you looking at the average family with two kids, they would pay about $400 in
       higher taxes.

9

Unit 3: SET UP something

STUDY THESE SENTENCES

The Red Cross **set up** a temporary shelter for the homeless.	1	build/put up a structure
He **set up** a meeting with his boss to discuss his ideas. GDI **set up** a website linked to a database of consumer products	2	make plans/establish something

IDIOMS

The company wanted to **set up shop** in London and New York	3	start or establish a new office or business

EXERCISES

A. Complete the sentences with the correct form of the verb *set*. If there are two blank spaces in the sentence, write *up* in the second space:

1. I hope he's not .... (set) himself .... for failure.
2. The state is aiming .... (set) a job-training program for high school dropouts.
3. Aviana is .... (set) a low-cost airline called Egg.
4. They contacted the creditors and .... (set) a payment plan.
5. He has already made enough money .... (set) himself .... for life.

B. Match the beginning of each sentence with the most suitable ending:

1. The insurance companies   set up a computer network in the offices.
2. The IT people   set up a conference call for Wednesday at 10a.m.
3. Judy is going to   setting up a telephone hotline.
4. The city is   set up a payment plan.
5. They contact the creditors and   set up mobile offices in Florida.

C. Correct the errors in these sentences. There is one error in each sentence:

1. The Internet Connection Wizard setted up my Internet connection.
2. Please setting up a meeting with Larry for Thursday at 9 a.m.
3. Using loans from the SBA, they set up shopping in Northern California.
4. The trick is to sets up an excellent marketing and distribution system.
5. Rockwell is in the process of set up a trade center.

Unit 4: CALL FOR something

STUDY THESE SENTENCES

The president **called for** an examination of high gas prices.	**1**	**ask for, demand**
The chairman will **call for** a board meeting in July.		
The agreement **calls for** the phone company to allow access to its networks.	**2**	**require**
Forecasts **call for** the dollar to fall against the yen.	**3**	**predict**
Analysts are **calling for** further declines in the price of copper		

EXERCISES

A. Using the information above, decide which use of *call for* is illustrated in each of the following examples. Write the number on the line:

1. The labor leaders called for a national strike. _____

2. The forecast calls for moderate growth in the GDP of about 1%. _____

3. The plan calls for the sale of the film production unit. _____

4. The plan calls for a 25% reduction in administrative costs. _____

B. Create full sentences using the words provided in the brackets and an appropriate form of *call on*. Include articles (the/a) with nouns where required. Answers may vary. The first one has been done for you:

1. (report/new restrictions/on/cigarette advertising)
   The report called for new restrictions on cigarette advertising.

2. (some shareholders/the resignation/of the/CEO)
   ....

3. (latest order/the supply/of/5/new/aircraft)
   ....

4. (manufacturers/a reduction/in/interest rates)
   ....

5. (average forecast/an overall gain/of/about 0.3%/in retail sales)
   ....

6. (new contract/ a 10% increase/ in salaries and bonuses)

....

7. (plan/ a 25% reduction/ in/ administrative costs)

....

This certainly calls for a celebration

Unit 5: REVIEW
DEAL WITH, LOOK AT, SET UP, CALL FOR

A. Select the phrasal verb that best completes the sentence:

1. The CFO is always .... the bottom line.
   (a) looking at   (b) looked at   (c) looks at

2. The harassment incidents were .... as they arose.
   (a) dealing with   (b) dealt with   (c) deal with

3. DDK is .... a 401(k) retirement plan for its employees.
   (a) set up   (b) sets up   (c) setting up

4. The US has .... the deregulation of Japan's insurance industry.
   (a) calling for   (b) call for   (c) called for

5. The retailer is going to .... an online store.
   (a) set up   (b) sets up   (c) setting up

B. Rewrite the sentences by replacing the underlined word or phrase with the correct form of the appropriate phrasal verb:

1. Procedures are in place to <u>handle</u> charges of discrimination or harassment.
2. I got a call from the guys in Denver. They want to <u>schedule</u> a meeting.
3. The study <u>examined</u> car thefts in metropolitan areas.
4. We are cutting back on the number of suppliers we <u>do business with</u>.
5. We started <u>considering</u> the idea of taking the company public.
6. My job is to <u>establish</u> a vitamin supply network in the US.
7. The new law <u>requires</u> tighter controls on the sharing of personal information.
8. Kuwait has abandoned a plan to <u>erect</u> a new oil refinery in Thailand.
9. The burger chain's latest plan <u>predicts</u> 3000 new restaurants world-wide.
10. The unions are <u>demanding</u> a strike against plans to privatize several state companies.

Unit 6: GO ON

STUDY THESE SENTENCES

OTHER PATTERNS go on (to) something

As time **goes on**, things will get better.	1	continue
The negotiations **went on** for two years.		carry on
A bidding war is **going on** between Boeing and Airbus.	2	occur, happen, take place
The staff were angry about what was **going on** in the company.		
Tom Brewster **went on** to business school, became a citizen, and eventually started a software company.	3	move on, continue
*Can we **go on** to page 10?*		
Frank **went on** (and on) about how much money he could have saved.	4	talk excessively, complain
The CEO **went on** TV to talk about the product recall..	5	appear on TV/radio

EXERCISES

A. Using the information above, decide which use of *go on* is illustrated in each of the following examples. Write the number on the line:

1. He is going on television to recruit franchisees. _____
2. Are you worried about what is going on in the economy? _____
3. He kept going on and on about his wife. _____
4. Many exporters go on to set up foreign operations. _____
5. On a day-to-day level, the work will go on as it has in the past. _____

B. Complete the sentences with a suitable form of *go on* (e.g., *is going on*) and one of the words from the box. Be sure to use the correct article (e.g. a/the) with the noun where required:

meetings	division	spokesperson	banking	in favor

1. Currently, there are a lot of mergers .... in the .... world.
2. Last night, the company's .... ABC's news program
3. There is a lively discussion .... between those .... of the changes and those who oppose the changes.
4. We don't know what .... in the finance ....··
5. I'm sure there will be some more .... as the week ....··

14

Unit 7: COME FROM

STUDY THESE SENTENCES

The main competition **comes from** Chinese factories.
The data **came from** DCI, a Washington trade group.
I **came from** a family of eight brothers and sisters.
Jim Hyde, a lawyer, **comes from** Michigan.

1   originate from

2   originate from
= place where you grew up

EXERCISES

A. Create full sentences using the words provided in the brackets and an appropriate form of *come from* (ex. *coming from*). Add articles (*a/the*) to the nouns where required: The first one has been done for you:

1. (participants/17 countries/including Japan, Russia, and Finland)
The participants come from 17 countries, including Japan, Russia, and Finland.
2. (70%/of /world's silk/China) ....
3. (impetus for change/new management team) .... :
4. (gas/Olmos Field/in Texas) ....
5. (savings/would/consolidating/10 offices) .... :

B. Complete the sentences with a suitable form of *come from* (e.g., *is coming from*) and one of the words from the box. Be sure to use the correct article (e.g. a/the) with the noun where required:

winning	entrepreneur	aid	surveys	statistics

1. The .... the NIH itself.
2. This unemployment figure .... house-to-house ....
3. The .... edge .... being the first on the block with information.
4. Some new help may .... the World Bank, the biggest single provider of
   ....
5. The speaker .... farthest away will be James Shaw, ...
   from Pennsylvania.

C. Correct the errors in these sentences. There is one error in each:

1. No one can imagine where such money will came from.
2. But his greatest challenge could coming from the peace process he helped forge.
3. These profits will come form the sale of housing units
4. 70 percent of the increased capital that has been available to Chinese banks since 1988 has came from individual deposits.

15

Unit 8: WORK ON something/someone

STUDY THESE SENTENCES

NASA is **working on** a new rocket.
The drug company is **working on** a new
 generation of Prozac-style drugs.
The company will **work on** reducing debt.

1   spend time on something

She has been **working on** me to join her
 volunteer group

2   try to persuade someone to do
         something

EXERCISES

A. Match the beginning of each sentence with the most suitable ending:

1. The architect is working
2. The pharmaceutical company has been working
3. The construction firm is working
4. We had been working
5. The chairperson was working

on them to change their policy.
on the idea that we'd reach an agreement this week.
on drugs to reduce blood pressure.
on a second condominium project.
on a new design for a skyscraper.

B. Create full sentences using the words provided in the brackets and an appropriate form of *work on*. Add articles (*a/the*) to the nouns where required. The first one has been done for you:

1. (industry researchers/ways of reducing the size of batteries)
   <u>Industry researchers are working on ways of reducing the size of batteries.</u>
2. (company/correcting the problem)
   ....:
3. (biotech company/cancer drug)
   ....:
4. (last fall/ad company/pro-smoking campaign/for Philip Morris)
   ....:
5. (I/assumption/meeting will take place very soon)
   ....
6. (company/said/it/software improvements)
   ....

C. Discussion Question

What kind of tasks or projects do you work on that require a lot of time and effort?

Unit 9: COME IN

STUDY THESE SENTENCES

We need to prevent drugs from **coming in** at the border.	1	enter
I **come in** every week for my paycheck		come in to work/the office
Results came in one cent a share above predictions.	2	enter, arrive, be introduced (data/results come in)
The new data **coming in** looks good		
The quarterly net income is likely to **come in** below expectations		
A call from head office came in for you while you were out		Email/calls/faxes come in
He **came in** as the new head of department.	3	join an organization/situation
He was disappointed to **come in** second in the competition.	4	=finish a race etc. in first/last/... position

IDIOMS

Lou's international experience will **come in handy** in his new job.	5	come in handy; come in useful =be useful
The plans have **come in for** a lot of criticism..	6	come in for criticism/blame/ abuse =be criticized/blamed/ abused, etc.

EXERCISES

A. Using the information above, decide which use of *come in* is illustrated in each of the following examples:

    1. Some calls came in from places like Hungary.   _____

    2. Thank you all for coming in this morning.   _____

    3. In the May ratings period, the television network came in third.   _____

    4. Judith Bridges will come in as president and CEO of the software company.

        _____

B. Complete the sentences with a suitable form of *come in* (e.g., *is coming in*) and one of the words from the box. Be sure to use the correct article (e.g. *a/the*) with the noun where required:

criticism	airports	checks	loan	management

1. More than 3000 flights _____ and out of New York _____ every day.
2. The accounting firm _____ for a lot of _____.
3. If the money doesn't _____, we'll have to take out _____.
4. _____ team _____ with a new plan during the last quarter.
5. We are waiting for _____ to _____.

C. Match the beginning of each sentence with the most suitable ending:

1. The US unemployment rate came   in, we can build up a better case.
2. The new models are coming   in late today.
3. As the evidence comes   in second in elections last fall.
4. I called and said I would be coming in at 6%.
5. The Independence Party came   in any day now.

D. Discussion Question

What item(s) would come in handy for the following situations?
(a) You become lost on your way to a business lunch.
(b) You have a headache.
(c) You are on a long flight overseas.
(d) You need to receive a fax, but you are away from the office.

Unit 10: REVIEW
GO ON, COME FROM, WORK ON, COME IN

A. Select the phrasal verb that best completes the sentence:

1. A fax from Jim .... this morning.
   (a) come in   (b) came in   (c) comes in

2. The false accounting .... for nearly two years.
   (a) went on   (b) go on   (c) goes on

3. We're .... a couple of deals right now.
   (a) worked on   (b) working on   (c) works on

4. Computers will have more power than regular game machines until next winter, when new systems .... Nintendo, Sega and Sony.
   (a) came from   (b) coming from   (c) come from

5. There are discussions .... with Enron about the use of the money.
   (a) coming from   (b) going on   (c) working on

B. Match the beginning of each sentence with the most appropriate ending:

1. US consumer data came in   to second careers
2. The fight has been going on   on target.
3. These days many people go on   for a number of years.
4. The computer retailer has been working on   everything is economics.
5. The world I come from,   a Hispanic marketing strategy

C. Rewrite the sentences by replacing the underlined word or phrase with the correct form of the appropriate phrasal verb:

1. After the hurricane, a large number of insurance claims are expected to <u>be filed</u>.
2. Hey, <u>what's happening</u>?
3. He is <u>writing</u> a book about globalization.
4. She <u>proceeded</u> to become one of the richest and most powerful women in the Arab world.
5. He said we should only accept funds that <u>originate from</u> federal taxes on products made here.

Corpus Lab Exercises 1

1. DEAL WITH

a.	The new leader will have to **deal with** the company's financial problems.
a.	All complaints are **dealt with** by a special committee.
b.	Anyone who **deals with** corrupt companies will be prosecuted.
c.	Have you seen the film **dealing with** the fall of Enron?
b.	We regularly **deal with** overseas companies.
a.	The toughest problem to **deal with** is the operating deficit.
c.	At the conference, half the presentations **dealt with** globalization

Give a synonym for the three meanings of *deal with* in the above sentences?

Meaning a. ....

Meaning b. ....

Meaning c. ....

2. One phrasal verb fits all the sentences. Which is it?

Are you worried about what is .... in the housing market?

The takeover talks .... for two months.

He kept .... and on about his bonus.

Many entrepreneurs .... to set up new companies.

He is .... television to promote the new product.

Phrasal verb ....

3. CALL FOR

1.	Johnson is calling for Copper prices to be as high as $4.
2.	He has called for advertisers to boycott the magazine.
3.	The new contract calls for workers to defer their wage increase for a year.
4.	A number of economists are calling for moderate GNP growth of about 2%.
5.	The Act calls for banks to make loans in low-income areas.
6.	MacDonald's expansion plans call for 2.500 to 3000 new restaurants worldwide

Assign each sentence to the appropriate meaning:

A. **predict**: Sentences ....

B. **ask for**: Sentences ....

C. **require**: Sentences ....

4. Concordance for SET UP

Look at the following concordance lines.

a. Four foreign manufacturers have **set up** shop here in the past ...
... members, the senate voted to **set up** a committee to study gambling. ...
takeover targets. The company has **set up** a committee to coordinate its ...
... more and more stores are **setting up** shop on the web. Some ...
.. hiring decisions, the president is **setting up** a committee to look into ...
went bankrupt. The accounting firm **set up** a fund to cover legal ...
... expansion plans, Nokia plans to **set up** a manufacturing facility in India. ...
cerning export licences, Mr. Haynes **set up** a meeting between executives and
... expansion program and wants to **set up** shop in Texas. It is ...
... contact with customers, P&G **set up** a toll-free hotline. Operators will ...
... our campaign, We need to **set up** a meeting with the marketing ...
he restaurant chain has traditionally **set up** shop in smaller towns, but ...
... damage, the company hopes to **set up** a meeting with FDA officials ...
... the Indian government is to **set up** a committee to review the ...
... more than $2 million to **set up** commercial websites over the last .

| 15 matches | Original text order | Strings matching: set* up |

Examine the phrasal verb *set up* in the center of each line and note which nouns follow the verb more than two times. The first one has been done for you.

shop........
set up   a ....
         a ....

5. One phrasal verb fits all the sentences. Which is it?

If more money doesn't .... soon we'll have to take out a loan
The sales .... about 50% ahead of last year's total
The faxed purchase order from E&Y .... this morning
When the sales data ...., we can see if we are on target.
I'll be .... late today.
The accounting firm for Enron .... for a lot of criticism.
Tony Chen will .... as CEO of the software company.

Phrasal verb ....

Unit 11: LOOK FOR something

STUDY THESE SENTENCES

John is **looking for** a new business to buy.   1   seek, try to find
A lot of laid-off managers are having to **look
 for** work again.

EXERCISES

A. Create full sentences using the words provided in the brackets and an appropriate
   form of *look for*. Add articles (*a/the*) to the nouns where required. The first one has
   been done for you:

1. (John/new business to buy)   John is looking for a new business to buy.
2. (phone company/new marketing strategies)

   ....

3. (a lot of/laid-off managers/must/work/again)

   ....

4. (advertisers/alternatives to TV and radio)

   ....

5. (Southcorp/plans to/growth in export markets/and in Asian ventures)

   ....

B. Complete the sentences with a suitable form of *look for* (e.g., *is looking for*) and one
   of the words from the box. Be sure to use the correct article (e.g. *a/the*) with the
   noun where required:

| buyers | construction | player | challenge | organizations |

1. In a new assistant director, the search committee .... someone who
   had experience working with service ....

2. Factories, palm oil and rubber plantations as well as .... companies,
   are forced to .... labor outside.

3. If we want to be .... in South East Asia, we must .... possible
   partnerships in Thailand and Korea.

4. Some .... say cost isn't the issue when they're .... quality.

5. Mr. Thomas said he was .... a new ....

Unit 12: DEPEND ON someone/something

STUDY THE EXAMPLES

I **depend on** Ryan for his sound advice.	1	rely on or trust someone
The company **depends on** Asia for 40% of its sales.	2	rely on something
Prices vary, **depending on** the model.	3	relating outcome/results to factors or a situation

EXERCISES

A. Using the information above, decide which meaning of *depend on* is illustrated in each of the following examples. Write the number on the line:

1. Mexico's future growth depends heavily on the US economy. _____
2. The price of oil depends upon a multitude of factors. _____
3. There are people depending on me and I don't want to let them down. _____
4. Rooms are $95 to $150 depending on demand. _____
5. Car companies depend heavily on foreign sales. _____

B. Match the beginning of each sentence with the most appropriate ending:

1. Depending on the type of hotel,
2. Success depends
3. We've been depending too much
4. Many local economies depend
5. What you make of the new information depends

on your perspective.
on Susan.
costs range from $50-$250.
on money from visitors.
on good products at reasonable prices.

C. Complete the sentences with a suitable form of *depend on* (e.g., *is depending on*) and the best choice of words from the box. Be sure to use the correct article (e.g. *a/the*) with the noun where required:

labels	farming	government	rates	sales

1. What happens next _____ entirely on _____.
2. Many consumers _____ food _____ for nutrition information.
3. Italy _____ _____ for 3% of its gross domestic product.
4. Mortgage _____ vary greatly _____ the product.
5. Our success _____ having a strong _____ team.

Unit 13: PICK UP something; PICK something up

STUDY THESE SENTENCES

I **picked** my tools **up** and started to work.	**1**	**get, lift something**
I **picked up** the phone.		(concrete object)
People often **pick up** colds and other illnesses at work.	**2**	**get something** (abstract object)
Even in a recession, we **picked up** market share.		
The economy is expected to **pick up** again next year.	**3**	**improve, increase**
Demand has **picked up** markedly since last year.		

IDIOMS

The government **picked up the** $12 million **tab**.	**4**	**pick up the tab** =pay for something
Investors are **picking up the pieces** after a week of volatile trading	**5**	**pick up the pieces** =deal with the consequences of a problem

EXERCISES

A. **Using the information above, decide which meaning of** *pick up* **is illustrated in each of the following examples. Write the number on the line:**

1. Dynergy will pick up the pieces from the collapse of Enron. _____
2. I need to pick up my suit before leaving on a business trip. _____
3. Who is going to pick up the tab for cleaning up the contaminated site? _____
4. Economists anticipate that economic growth will pick up this year. _____
5. The car company was confident that it could pick up market share. _____

B. **Match the beginning of each sentence with the most appropriate ending:**

1. I picked up	because of the high dollar.
2. Exports did not pick up	steam.
3. He picked up	the phone and called my supervisor.
4. The online gambling industry is picking up	the pieces.
5. After a bankruptcy someone has to pick up	the tab for the meal.

Unit 14: MEET WITH someone/something

STUDY THESE SENTENCES

Last week the Chief Financial Officer **met with** analysts.

1   **meet** (for business or discussions)

The proposal is certain to **meet with** protests from the unions.

2   =a focus on the reactions to or consequences of something

EXERCISES

A. For each sentence decide if *meet with* refers to (1) *meeting as a result of planning* or
    (2) *reactions or consequences* and write the number on the line.

1. His efforts met with only limited success.
2. When you have gathered all the information, you are ready to meet with your boss.
3. The lawyers met with hospital officials.
4. The proposals met with opposition from some importers.
5. Bad results from the company are not met with surprise these days.

B. The following sentences illustrate the use of *meet with* in terms of reactions or consequences:

1. The marketing campaign has met with limited success so far.
2. The mayor is hopeful that the new policies will meet with public approval.
3. The company's proposal met with harsh criticism.
4. Attempts to introduce a set of revised rules met with vigorous opposition.
5. His claims were met with utter disbelief.
6. Talk of the merger was met with cautious optimism.

Reread the sentences, then fill in the chart to show which sorts of words collocate with *meet with*. Decide which collocations have a negative connotation. The first has been done for you:

X	form of *meet with*	Y	Negative connotation?
marketing campaign	has met with	limited success	yes

Unit 15: REVIEW
LOOK FOR, DEPEND ON, PICK UP, MEET WITH

A. Select the phrasal verb that best completes this sentence:

1. The fund is .... companies that have high growth potential.
   (a) look for   (b) looks for   (c) looking for   (d) looked for

2. If possible, I would like to .... you and discuss my plans for the future.
   (a) meets with   (b) meet with   (c) meeting with   (d) met with

3. He is able to .... the phone and make a call to the CEO.
   (a) picked up   (b) picking up   (c) pick up   (d) picks up

4. The just-in-time approach .... the components arriving on time.
   (a) depend on   (b) depending on   (c) depends on   (d) depend

B. Replace the underlined word or phrase with the appropriate phrasal verb. Be sure to use the correct form of the verb:

1. The company paid the tab for a 3-day retreat in Colorado.
2. Profits will be good if the property market improves.
3. Local TV stations rely on news programming for a large portion of their revenue.
4. We're always researching ways to make our products better.
5. I'm gonna see the accounting people today.

C. Rewrite the sentences by replacing the underlined word or phrase with the correct form of *pick up* (e.g. *is picking up*).

1. The government may pay for some of the health costs of early retirees.
2. Demand for gasoline has increased sharply in the last month.
3. Luckily, sales improved later in the season.
4. If you look at any magazine, you see a variety of diet ads.

D. Answer yes or no to the following questions:

1. If the Asian telephone market is picking up speed, is it improving?
2. If I am looking for a position in the Bay Area, am I searching for a job?
3. If US taxpayers have to pick up the tab for the new security measures, does this mean they will have to pay for them?
4. If executives got together with employees to explain the new pension plan, did they meet?
5. If the market fails to pick up, does it improve?

Unit 16: MAKE UP something

STUDY THESE SENTENCES

OTHER PATTERNS make something up

Sales to Japan **make up** 90% of the company's international business.	1	comprise, amount to
We can easily **make up** a customer survey. The jury decided the story was a hoax and that he **made** the whole thing **up.**	2	invent, create (sometimes in order to deceive)
McQueen said that town hall has offered to **make up** if he signs a document promising not to speak to the press about the local scandal.	3	become friendly again after a fight
California still hasn't **made up** for jobs lost in the last recession.	4	add enough of something to reach a target

IDIOMS

I **made up my mind** to get back into sales.	5	make up my mind =decide
Boeing told NASA that it could **make up for lost time**	6	make up for lost time =do something to compensate for lost time

EXERCISES

A. Rewrite the sentences by replacing the underlined word with a suitable form of *make up* (e.g. *is making up*):

1. Oil comprises 25 percent of Venezuela's gross domestic product.
2. We don't know how much money we lost because the numbers were fabricated.
3. I decided to learn something about computers.
4. The phone company will compensate for lost income by charging higher rates.
5. He invested less than $100 to advertise in a local paper and created some fliers.

B. These sentences illustrate some of the collocations for *make up*. Match the beginning of each sentence with the most suitable ending:

1. Many voters made up	a story that I was stealing from the firm.
2. I'll make up	10% of the country's supply.
3. Boeing told NASA that it could make up	some packets for the conference attendees.
4. The partner made up	their mind a long time ago.
5. Solar power makes up	for lost time on the space project.

27

Unit 17: DO WITH something

STUDY THESE SENTENCES

She loved anything to **do with** sports. The changeable weather has something to **do with** global warming. Mark says he wants **nothing to do with** stolen merchandise.	**1**	**connected with, related to**

EXPLANATION

Examples   Meteorologists say that the changeable weather has **something to do with** global warming.

Meaning   Global warming is connected to the changeable weather, but meteorologists are not sure exactly how.

Examples   My resignation has **nothing to do with** the company's current problems.

Meaning   The fact that the company has problems is not the reason for resigning.

CORPUS NOTE: Strong pattern:
... have nothing/something/anything to do with ...
... has to do with ...

EXERCISES

A. Choose a word from the box to best complete the sentences:

safety	finances	it	drop	goal

1. I have a question. It has to do with the overall .... of the report.
2. The cost-cutting has nothing to do with the .... of the airline
3. Mr. Stewart said he has nothing to do with his wife's ....
4. Pride may have a lot to do with ....
5. The high price of oil has little to do with the .... in share prices.

B. Circle the correct word to complete the sentences:

1. Most banks don't want (anything/nothing) to do with the credit card company.
2. I had (anything/nothing) to do with the PPM deal.
3. I know he didn't have (anything/nothing) to do with it.
4. The dispute has (anything/nothing) to do with us.
5. RTL TV said the change had (anything/nothing) to do with complaints.

Unit 18: ACCOUNT FOR something

STUDY THESE SENTENCES

Energy trading may soon **account for** more than 10% of Texaco's earnings	1	**make up a proportion or percentage**
The manager said the costs were **accounted for** in the revised budget.	2	if something is *accounted for* it is included in an accounting system or budget
The structural problems **accounted for** the current crisis in the industry..	3	explain

EXERCISES

A. **Using the information above, decide which use of *account for* is illustrated in each of the following examples. Write the number on the line:**

   1. The popular brand accounted for 56% of the company's operating profit last
       year.   _____
   2. Traders said there was no major news to account for the dollar's gains.   _____
   3. The men could be brought before a federal grand jury to account for their
       conduct.   _____
   4. Kitchens and baths account for about one-third of total remodeling expenditures.
                                                                                  _____
   5. All budget adjustments should be accounted for.   _____

B. **Create full sentences using the words provided in the brackets and the correct form of *account for*. Add articles (*a/the*) to the nouns where required. The first one has been done for you:**

   1. (sugar/one third/of Fiji's exports)   Sugar accounts for one third of Fiji's
      exports.
   2. (windmills/about 3500 megawatts/of electricity/in US)

      ....
   3. (Deutsche Telekom/about 96 percent/of telephone sales/in Germany)

      ....
   4. (memory chips/more than 60%/of/company's profit/in 2002)

      ....
   5. (reports/did not/connection/ between/cases)

      ....

Unit 19:RELY ON someone/something

STUDY THESE SENTENCES

Brazil **relies on** gas for only 3% of its fuel needs.
PKC has **relied on** high-cost funds borrowed from banks.
The exporters **relied on** government help.
The company **relied on** its financial advisers.
*You can **rely on** us to give you the best price.*

1   **depend on something**

2   **depend on someone**

EXERCISES

A. Match the beginning of each sentence with the most appropriate ending:

1. The company's strategy is to rely

   on rental income to meet their operating and maintenance expenses

2. Housing authorities rely

   solely on conventional marketing techniques

3. I relied

   on cartridge games while the Sony PlayStation will play compact disc-based games.

4. Retailers these days don't rely

   on acquisitions to achieve double-digit growth

5. Nintendo's Ultra 64 will still rely

   on the advice of financial professionals.

B. Complete the sentences with a suitable form of *rely on* (e.g., *is relying on*) and one of the words from the box. Be sure to use the correct article (e.g. *a/the*) with the noun where required:

company	development	customers	market	fuel

1. The Korean .... is small and so electronics companies .... exports.
2. For many years auto companies have .... cash rebates to attract ....:
3. We can't .... other companies to do our research and .... for us.
4. Brazil .... gas for only 3% of its .... needs.
5. .... should be able to .... digital cameras, its traditional cash cow.

30

Unit 20: REVIEW
MAKE UP, DO WITH, ACCOUNT FOR, RELY ON

A. **Select the phrasal verb that best completes this sentence:**

1. Technology stocks .... a considerable portion of the NASDAQ index.
   (a) makes up   (b) making up   (c) make up   (d) is made up

2. If exports can't .... the rise in profits, what is the motivating factor?
   (a) accounted for (b) accounting for   (c) accounts for   (d) account for

3. The judge dismissed a portion of the case in which Virgin Atlantic ....
   state laws.
   (a) relying on   (b) relied on   (c) is relied on   (d) is rely on

4. ``I believe I can do it, and believing in yourself has a lot to .... it.''
   (a) do with   (b) does with   (c) doing with   (d) did with

B. **Replace the underlined word or phrase with the appropriate phrasal verb. Be sure to use the correct form of the verb:**

1. It is estimated that packaging costs <u>comprise</u> about half the total cost of making soft-drink products.
2. "I still <u>need</u> her every day," he said.
3. In the past, the exports <u>depended on</u> the Hong Kong and Macao markets.
4. The reason for the delay <u>is involved with</u> production difficulties.
5. Officials were unable to immediately <u>explain</u> what caused the machine to malfunction.

C. **Answer yes/no to the question that follows each statement:**

1. PKC has relied on high-cost funds borrowed from banks. Has the company depended on borrowing?

2. Initially, the venture will rely on the parent company for financing. Will the venture need financing from the parent company?

3. The error had nothing to do with the level of actual gains or losses in the fund. Is the error is to blame for the changes in the fund?

4. We worked through much of the night to make up for lost time. Were the workers trying to compensate for time passed?

5. Mexican producers rely on imported parts and raw materials. Do the producers need imported parts and raw materials?

CorpusLab Exercises 2

1. Phrasal Verbs based on WITH
Fill in the blank with the appropriate form of *do, deal,* or *meet*.

1. We may have to .... with a lawsuit.
2. The proposals .... with opposition from some importers.
3. The company's marketing campaign has .... with limited success so far.
4. The dispute has nothing to .... with us.
5. We have .... with analysts to discuss the company's performance.
6. People .... with stress in different ways.

2. One phrasal verb fits all the sentences. Which is it?

Sales and distribution costs .... about one-third of the retail price of a car.
Officials were unable to .... what caused the machine to malfunction.
Sugar .... one third of Fiji's exports.
Packaging costs .... about half the total cost of making soft-drink products.
Traders said there was no major news to .... the dollar's gains.

Phrasal verb ....

3. PICK UP

1.	The car company is confident that it can pick up market share.
2.	I need to pick up my suit before leaving on a business trip.
3.	Can you pick me up at the hotel?
4.	Profits will be good if the property market picks up.
5.	Economists anticipate that economic growth will pick up this year.
6.	Demand for gasoline has picked up sharply in the last month.
7.	We picked up a fair amount of business at the tradeshow

Assign each sentence to the appropriate meaning:
   A. **get, lift, collect**   Sentences _____
   B. **get (something abstract:** Sentences _____
   C. **improve, increase:**   Sentences _____

4. One phrasal verb fits all the sentences. Which is it?

Solar power .... 10% of the country's supply.
We worked through much of the night to .... for lost time.
The phone company will .... for lost income by charging higher rates.
There is still time to .... lost ground.
Servers .... around 20% of the computer company's sales.

Phrasal verb ....

5. Concordance for MEET WITH

Look at the following concordance lines.

nting people today . The lawyers **met with** hospital officials. The proposals m
h hospital officials. The proposals **met with** opposition from some importers.
m some importers. The president **met with** investment bankers to explore a .
npany's marketing campaign has **met with** limited success so far. Executives .
limited success so far. Executives **met with** employees to explain the new ...
... possible, I would like to **meet with** you and discuss my plans ...
... from the company are not **met with** surprise these days. Solar power .
... respond to your offer to **meet with** Mr. Belden to discuss potential ...
e the merger announcement, was **met with** warm applause and made some ..
... Any talk of deregulation is **met with** a lot of opposition, and ...
... with a rights issue were **met with** little enthusiasm by investors. The
... be more than happy to **meet with** your client at the appropriate ...

50 matches	Original text order	Strings matching: me%t with

Look at the center of line where meet with is displayed. Next look at the following words, the object of the phrasal verb. You can see that the objects in the first and second lines are very different. The object in the first line refers to people, *hospital officials*; the object in the second line is a reaction or xxxx, *opposition*. List all the examples of reaction

	REACTION			PERSON
meet with	opposition		meet with	hospital officials
	....			....
	....			....
	....			....
	....			....
	....			....

6. One phrasal verb fits all the sentences. Which is it?

John is .... a new business to buy.
The fund is .... companies that have high growth potential.
A lot of laid-off managers are having to .... work again.
Thomas said he was .... a new challenge.
We're always .... ways to make our products better

Phrasal verb ....

Unit 21: TAKE OVER something

STUDY THESE SENTENCES

Enron was **taken over** by its smaller rival Dynergy.

It is likely that Dynergy will **take** Enron **over**.

Jennings will **take over** as chairman in January.	1	buy, take control of a company
	2	start a job or task, take up a leadership position

EXERCISES

A. Using the information above, decide which use of *take over* is illustrated in each of the following examples. Write the number on the line:

1. The Japanese partner will take over most of the work. _____
2. Ms. Jennings will take over as CFO on July 1. _____
3. Aerospace Industries was taken over by Hughes Electronics. _____
4. He will take over responsibility for investment strategy. _____
5. The company made a hostile bid to take over Unitron. _____

B. Complete the sentences with a suitable form of *take over* (e.g., *is taking over*) and one of the words from the box. Be sure to use the correct article (e.g. *a/the*) with the noun where required:

reorganization	regulators	management firm	reports	company

1. Rupert Morley has run _____ well since he _____ in 2002.
2. San Diego's HomeFed bank was _____ by _____ in 1992.
3. VCS Bank denied Dutch press _____ that it plans to _____ Credit Lyonnais Bank.
4. Under _____, some areas will be increasingly _____ by representatives working in the field.
5. _____ will _____ day-to-day operations from the founder and CEO.

C. Discussion Question

1. Should the government take over responsibility for health care?

Unit 22: POINT OUT someone/something

STUDY THESE SENTENCES

OTHER PATTERNS point something/someone out

He **pointed out** the homes of Silicon Valley CEOs.	1	physically identify someone/something
The report **points out** some encouraging aspects of the Indian economy.	2	highlights, draw attention to something

EXERCISES

A. Select the correct form of *point out* to complete the sentence:

1. She .... that IPOs nearly doubled in 2003.
(a) pointing out   (b) point out   (c) points out

2. Company officials .... they have hired 18,500 new workers over the last four years.
(a) point out   (b) pointing out   (c) points out

3. Some analysts .... that the year-over-year gains are not so impressive, considering last year's low earnings.
(a) pointing out   (b) points out   (c) point out

PROJECTED SALES = $100,000
COSTS = $85,000
PROFIT= $25,000

EXPORT CHINA
OUTSOURCING

Can I point out a small problem?

B. Rewrite the sentences by replacing the underlined word or phrase with a correct form of *point out* (e.g. *is pointing out*).

1. The company <u>says</u> it didn't start the strike, which affected workers in three states.

2. Industry experts <u>claim</u> that the car company has far to go to catch with industry standards for efficiency.

3. I would just <u>add</u> that I see an adjustment to house prices as the most significant risk here.

4. Mr. Rivlin <u>showed</u> that deficit naturally rises during times of economic slack

5. A: It's 12.05.
    B: Thank you Robert for <u>bringing that to our attention</u>.

Unit 23: GIVE UP (doing) something

STUDY THESE SENTENCES

We haven't **given up**, but it will be hard to win the competition.	1	surrender, admit you cannot do something (similar to *give in*)
He is trying to **give up** smoking.	2	stop having, using, or doing something
He **gave up** his American citizenship and went back to India.		

EXERCISES

A. Rewrite the sentences by replacing the underlined word or phrase with the correct form of *give up* (e.g. *is giving up*):

1. He <u>ended</u> his academic career to focus on finance.
2. We had no choice but to keep going. We couldn't <u>surrender</u>.
3. If we borrow more money we will be <u>losing</u> equity in the company.
4. I love farming; I wouldn't <u>stop doing it</u> for anything.
5. You should never <u>lose</u> hope.

B. Create full sentences using the words provided in the brackets and an appropriate form of *give up*. Be sure to use the correct article (e.g. *a/the*) with the nouns where required. The first one has been done for you:

1. (career in politics/spend more time with his family)
 He gave up a career in politics to spend more time with his family.

2. (photography/join the army)
 ----

3. (her free time/help new immigrants)
 ----

4. (millions of Americans/cigarettes)
 ----

5. (dollar/yesterday's gains/ against/euro)

Unit 24: END UP somewhere

STUDY THESE SENTENCES

OTHER PATTERNS end up doing something
His family fled the country and **ended up** in   1   **come to be in a place or**
  the US.   **situation**
I ended up working as a dishwasher.

EXERCISES

A. **Match the beginning of each sentence with the most suitable ending. There may be
more than one correct answer in some cases:**

1. Some regions such as California could	end up issuing stock to repay borrowed money.
2. The company may	end up not having enough supplies of electric power.
3. I understand that we could	we could end up unemployed.
4. If we don't win another large contract,	end up costing the company around $300 million.
5. The strike will	end up collecting less than 100% of what we are owed.

B. **Complete the sentences with a suitable form of *end up* (e.g., *ended up*) and one of the
words/phrases from the box. Be sure to use the correct article (e.g. *a/the*) with the
nouns where required:**

careful	scheme	entire charges	surplus	moved

1. The company .... settling .... by paying a small fine.
2. If we're not ...., we'll .... in debt
3. He .... to Manhattan and finally .... working in Los Angeles.
4. The city government may .... with .... of unspent money.
5. .... may .... costing as much as $20 billion.

Unit 25: REVIEW
TAKE OVER, POINT OUT, GIVE UP, END UP

A. Select the phrasal verb that best completes each sentence:

1. Greg Wolf .... as chief operating officer from Mr. Tyson.
   (a) pointed out   (b) took over (c) gave up   (d) ended up

2. On Tuesday, the stock market .... closing 6.26 percent lower.
   (a) pointed out   (b) gave up   (c) ended up (d) took over

3. The Lloyds' agents never .... their right to sue in U.S. courts.
   (a) points out   (b) ended up   (c) took over   (d) gave up

4. If you don't correct the mistakes now, you're going to .... having to correct them in six months to a year.
   (a) end up   (b) point out   (c) gave up   (d) taking over

5. The analyst .... that the companies price-to-earnings ratio is about 10% higher than its expected growth rate.
   (a) takes over   (b) gives up   (c) points out   (d) ends up

B. Match the beginning of each sentence with the most suitable ending:

1. A veteran Japanese diplomat has	ended up pretty much where it started the year.
2. The market	pointed out the restrictions in the contracts.
3. If you withdraw money from a retirement plan	but we are not going to give up.
4. The Saatchi firm	taken over as executive director.
5. It is a David and Goliath battle,	you give up future tax- exempt growth.

Unit 26: SPIN OFF something

STUDY THESE SENTENCES

CF says it will **spin off** a major transportation subsidiary into a separate company.

1 **separate, make a part of a company into a completely new company**

EXERCISES

A. Choose the correct form of *spin off* to complete the sentences:

1. Bally Entertainment _____ Bally Total Fitness in 1999.
   (a) spin off   (b) spun off   (c) is spinning off

2. Highway Express was _____ from Transport Services Inc.
   (a) spin off   (b) spun off   (c) spinning off

3. The chairman refused to discuss whether the company will _____ any of its new holdings.
   (a) spin off   (b) spun off   (c) spinning off

4. Payton is being _____ by Quality Department Stores Co.
   (a) spin off   (b) spun off   (c) spinning off

5. Viacom is unlikely to _____ Blockbuster any time soon.
   (a) spin off   (b) spun off   (c) spinning off

B. Match the beginning of each sentence with the most suitable ending.

1. K-C plans to spin off its cigarette-paper   its auto-finance unit.
2. Sprint is going to spin off   to spin off its casino holdings.
3. The company will spin off   its banking operations to
                                                         shareholders.
4. The hotel chain announced that it plans   and tobacco operations.
5. Ford might spin off   its cellular operations.

Unit 27: ENTER INTO something

STUDY THESE SENTENCES

EGM **entered into** a five-year marketing services agreement with the AC Group. The two companies will **enter into** a joint sales and marketing agreement.

1 agree to, enter into something (ex. an agreement or arrangement), take part in something

EXERCISES

A. Choose the correct form of *enter into* to complete the sentences:

1. The corporation has .... an agreement with YBG for the sale of the manufacturing unit.
   (a) entering into   (b) entered into   (c) enter into
2. EGM .... a five-year marketing services agreement with the AC Group.
   (a) entering into   (b) enter into   (c) entered into
3. The company wants to .... long term strategic arrangements within the Western region.
   (a) entering into   (b) entered into   (c) enter into

B. These sentences illustrate some of the collocations for *enter into*. For each sentence, underline the noun phrase that follows the phrasal verb then use the information to complete the list of patterns below. The first one has been done for you.

1. TR Corp has **entered into** <u>an oil and gas exploration agreement</u> with LDN Gas Corp.
2. SPIC has entered into a strategic alliance with EGM to jointly promote various financial products.
3. The Canadian subsidiary said it has entered into negotiations with Gem World.
4. The company has entered into tentative deals to build two new office blocks.
5. Gas Corp. has entered into financial contracts, allowing it to sell natural gas at set prices.
6. The US companies often enter into partnerships with Chinese or Hong Kong counterparts.
7. The sales data are entered into the computer every day.
8. Sign up and you will be entered into a drawing for concert tickets.

Patterns:
Enter into an agreement

....

....

....

....

Unit 28: COME UP

STUDY THESE SENTENCES

Marilyn **came up** two flights of stairs to my apartment.
She had **come up** from Houston for the event.

1 Basic meaning: movement
  (a) from a lower physical (geographical) location to a higher location

People **come up** to me to ask for my autograph.

  (b) toward somebody or something (=approach)

After Windows **comes up** on the screen, the computer freezes.

2 Extended meanings:
  (a) emerge/rise/appear
  = appear

The election is **coming up** in November.

  = take place in the future

Mr. Thompson has **come up** quickly through the organization to become CEO.
She has certainly **come up** in the world since her days as a waitress.

  = advance/be promoted at work

Did my name **come up** in the meeting?
The question of money never **came up** again.

  (b) mentioned/discussed in conversation

I won't be able to make the meeting; something's **come up**.

  (c) happened unexpectedly

IDIOMS

The police **came up empty-handed** in their search for the suspect.

3 come up empty-handed
  = to not find something or to be unsuccessful in something you are doing

The company wanted to take over the bank, but had **come up short** with its $12 billion offer.

4 come up short
  = close to reaching a goal, but unsuccessful; fail to reach a goal

RELATED PHRASAL VERBS

The consultants **came up with** a plan to save the company.
A New York businessman has four weeks **to come up with** $4 million..

  come up with
5 produce a plan/proposal/idea

  make arrangements to obtain a particular sum of money

EXERCISES

A. Using the information above, decide which use of *come up* is illustrated in each of the following examples. Write the number on the line (ex. 1 (a), 2 (c), etc.):

1. My fifth anniversary with the company is coming up this Friday.   _____
2. He has the strength and energy – that's what enabled him to come up this far.

   _____

3. There are some interesting products downstairs that I had a chance to look at before coming up here.   _____
4. One issue that came up was the use of security cameras.   _____
5. How did they come up with the cash to do the deal?   _____
6. Make sure the server comes up after the reboot.   _____

B. Replace the underlined word or phrase with an appropriate form of *come up*:

1. We <u>created</u> the chocolate theme for the ad.
2. A. Are we in on this?
   B. Yeah, your name <u>appears</u>.
3. You gotta give me another week to <u>find</u> $1000.
4. Our employees <u>produced</u> the best selling product.
5. There's a couple of bond deals <u>taking place soon</u>.

C. Complete the sentences with a suitable form of *come up* (e.g., *is coming up*) and one of the words from the box. Be sure to use the correct article (e.g. *a/the*) with the noun where required:

them	plan	Hispanics	it	wedding

1. That's great that your brother's .... is ....
2. You're going to have problems and it is worthwhile to deal with .... as they ....
3. We .... with the magazine to target .... who were born in the US.
4. A. What about the finance problem?
   B. If it ...., just say that we're working on ....
5. Let me .... with .... and I'll get back with you early next week.

Unit 29: BUILD UP something

STUDY THESE SENTENCES

*We spent five years **building up** our business*   1   increase, grow
in California.

EXERCISES

A. Rewrite the sentences by replacing the underlined word or phrase with the correct form of *build up* (e.g. *is building up*):

1. The computer manufacturer may have <u>accumulated</u> too much inventory of memory chips.
2. We have <u>established</u> our internet operations over the last two years.
3. He acquired the company in 1990 and <u>developed it</u> over the following decade.
4. American Airlines have been trying to <u>add to</u> their business in Asia.
5. MTG has hired a consultant to <u>strengthen</u> its Canadian operations.

B. Complete the sentences with a suitable form of *build up* (e.g., *is building up*) and one of the words from the box. Be sure to use the correct article (e.g. a/the) with the noun where required:

inventories   loyal customer base   automaker   holdings   backlog

1. Investors .... their .... of foreign stocks.
2. .... of orders has .... for the popular game machine.
3. The supermarket is gradually ....
4. Companies reduced their .... in May after .... them .... in April.
5. .... sells its latest car at a loss to .... market share.

C. Discussion Questions

1. How does a company build up a good client base?
2. Have you built up any vacation time this year? If so, are you planning to take a trip?

Unit 30: REVIEW
SPIN OFF, ENTER INTO, COME UP, BUILD UP

A. Select the phrasal verb that best completes the sentence:

1. The bank has failed to .... with a solution to the loan dispute with ACG.
   (a) coming up   (b) came up   (c) come up

2. Because of the fall in earning, plans to .... units have been postponed.
   (a) spins off   (b) spinning off   (c) spin off

3. The partnerships .... complex financing and hedging arrangements with Neron.
   (a) entered into   (b) is entering into   (c) enters into

4. Let me .... with a plan and get back to you next week.
   (a) came up   (b) come up   (c) coming up

5. RWE has .... a derivatives trading team.
   (a) built up   (b) building up   (c) builds up

B. Match the beginning of each sentence with the most appropriate ending:

1. We need to come up with   a new set of numbers based on projected expenditures.

2. You gotta give me another week to   build up our marketing operations.
3. It will take a couple of years to   build up its sales force.
4. The company will use the capital to   you will not be allowed in the building.

5. If you try to come up here,   come up with the $500.

C. Rewrite the sentences by replacing the underlined word or phrase with the correct form of the appropriate phrasal verb:

1. The board is meeting to decide whether to sell the cable unit or instead offshoot it as an independent company.

2. The company may have to get its hands on more money to honor a collateral call on a $600 million note.

3. EMG has arranged a five-year marketing services agreement with ACG.

4. Neron has established an agreement with Warburg for the sale of Netcom.

5. The management will not agree to a transaction that might threaten the company's stability.

CorpusLab Exercises 3

1. Phrasal Verbs based on UP
Fill in the blank with the appropriate form of *set, make, build, come, end* or *give*.

1. The automaker sells its latest car at a loss to .... up market share.
2. One question that .... up was the use of security cameras.
3. They want to .... up a conference call to discuss earnings.
4. The utility company could .... up fighting three separate legal battles.
5. ADG eventually .... up on its strategy and sold its credit unit to a merchant bank
6. The company will use the capital to .... up its sales force.
7. Exports .... up 20% of overall revenue.
8. I really need to .... up working in a fast food restaurant.
9. If you try to .... up here, you will not be allowed in the building.
10. He invested less than $100 to advertise and .... up some fliers
11. GreenPow .... up shop as alternative energy suppliers.
12. If you put all your eggs in a basket, you .... up with a big mess.

2. One phrasal verb fits all the sentences. Which is it?

He .... that the outlook for Neron was "not very favorable".
She gives tours of LA .... the homes of the stars.
Sharon .... that 80% of the Morgan Stanley hiring is from internships.
Thank you for .... that ....
Terry .... the new CFO.

Phrasal verb ....

3. Give the missing collocations in the following sentences

1. Please set up a .... with Larry for Thursday at 9am.
2. We're far behind schedule; we need to make up for lost ....
3. How did they come up with the .... to pay off their debts.
4. We need to come up with a .... to save the company
5. If we spend more than we earn, we'll end up in ....
6. Did the .... payment come up.

4. COME UP

1.	Banking officials could not come up with hard data to support the claim.
2.	The web server will come up again soon.
3.	Did the issue of payment come up at the meeting?
4.	Let me come up with a plan and get back to you..
5.	Could you come up to reception?
6.	You must come up and see us next time
7.	Did my name come up?

Assign each sentence to the appropriate meaning:
A. **approach**   Sentences ....
B. **arise/emerge/start** Sentences ....
C. **produce:**   Sentences ....
D **be mentioned:**   Sentences ....

5. Concordance for ENTER INTO

Look at the following concordance lines.

dependent company. Neron has **entered into** an agreement with Warburg for
effort focused on identifying and **enter into** agreements in the Eastern region
ACG. The management will not **enter into** a transaction that might threaten
States and KWI in Europe have **entered into** a 'war of words' regarding which
Parallel to this deal, Enron also **entered into** a separate agreement with HMS
offer by EnronOnline or Enron to **enter into** any transaction on those or any of
s is due to power contracts PGE **entered into** at prices that were significantly l
ed States, announced that it has **entered into** a strategic alliance with Enron G
it Union by November 15 to be **entered into** a contest to win a Palm Vx! Log
all aware, Enron and UBS have **entered into** an agreement for the sale of cert.
Colleague: On Thursday, Enron **entered into** a settlement over Dynegy's exerc
inantly commodity transactions **entered into** with 'large financial institutions'

30 matches	Original text order	Strings matching: enter* into

Examine the phrasal verb *enter into* in the center of each line and note the frequent noun objects. (If the verb is passive, the object precedes the verb.)

enter into   ....
                    ....
                    ....

46

Unit 31: SHUT DOWN something

STUDY THESE SENTENCES

North Korea promised to **shut down** an old
 nuclear reactor.
Hurricane Dean **shut down** operations for
 three days.

1   stop operating, close down

EXERCISES

A. Match the beginning of each sentence with the most appropriate ending:

1. Unemployment will rise
2. Financial markers will shut down
3. The plant was shut down
4. The strike shut down
5. She shut down her computer

for two days due to public holidays.
when inefficient industries are shut down.
when the meeting started.
one assembly plant in Michigan.
when a leak in a pipe was discovered.

B. Create full sentences using the words provided in the brackets and an appropriate form of *shut down*. Include articles (the/a) with nouns where required. Answers may vary. The first one has been done for you:

1. (refinery / after / leak was detected)
   The refinery was shut down after a leak was detected.

2. (Araco Inc. / decided / its / zinc mine / in Colorado)
   ....

3. (investment-management unit / last week).
   ....

4. (Wall Corp / plans to / metal-can production facility / in Ohio)
   ....

5. (strike / car and truck / assembly lines).
   ....

C. Discussion Questions

1. Do you think music-sharing websites should be shut down? How about movie-sharing websites?
2. Should industrial plants be forced to shut down if they do not meet anti-air pollution policies?

Unit 32: SPECIALIZE IN (doing) something

STUDY THESE SENTENCES

Mr. Lee **specialized in** exporting to Asian countries Browne Woods is a New York brokerage firm, **specializing in** banks.	**1 concentrate on, focus on, have expertise in**

EXERCISES

A. Complete the sentences with a suitable form of *specialize in* (e.g., *is specializing in*) and the best choice of words from the box. Be sure to use the correct article (e.g. *a/the*) with the noun where required:

initiatives	staff	real estate	restructuring	management

1. ATS, which has offices in seven states, ... providing temporary office ....
2. Joel Scott is a turnaround expert who .... large companies.

3. Apple Computer plans several .... aimed at promoting sales by resellers who .... Apple products.
4. Mr. Steinberger is .... consultant at BHW where he .... book publishing projects.
5. Georgia Properties is .... investment trust, ... south-east apartments.

B. Discussion Question

1. Name a company then state the company's specialty. Be sure to use a correct form of *specialize in* to complete the sentence. For example, *Quanta Services is a contracting firm that specializes in building and maintaining infrastructure.*

Do you specialize in mergers?

UNIT 33: FIND OUT something

STUDY THESE SENTENCES

I want to **find out** how much the new DVD players cost.

Doing business in that country is not always easy; my company **found** that **out**.

1 discover
   (a) (find out something)

   (b) (find something out)

EXERCISES

A. **Complete the sentences with the correct form of *find* and the particle *out*. If there is one blank space, then write the verb and particle together.**

1. Business travel can be difficult. My boss .... that .... when he visited Iceland.
2. When I .... what the deal is, I'll let you know.
3. Companies .... that they could cut costs by hiring temporary workers.
4. I .... the hard way that stocks can go down as well as up.
5. Did you take the time to .... if they had insurance?

B. **Study the patterns below then add to the lists:**

(a) find out X	(b) find out what...	(c) find out if...	(d) find out how...
the price	the client needs	he read the report	much it will cost
....	....	....	....
....	....	....	....
....	....	....	....

C. **Discussion Questions**

Find out new information. Use the newspaper or web to answer these questions:

1. If you need to find out the weather forecast for your upcoming business trip, check here:

2. If you want to find out mortgage rates, check here:

3. If you want to find out how your stocks are doing, look here:

4. If you want to find out the latest currency exchange rates, check here:

UNIT 34: PUT IN (something); PUT (something) IN

STUDY THESE SENTENCES

The government wants to encourage workers to put money in a pension plan.	1	**place** something **in** something
She **puts in** fewer than 100 hours a month at the office.	2	spend time/effort
The office manager **put in** an order for 10 new computers.	3	submit order/request, etc.
The new machines will be put in service next year.	4	install

IDIOMS

Sandy was **put in charge of** the West Coast office.	5	put in charge of = make someone the head / the leader
The NASDAQ has put in place a series of changes.	6	put in place = establish

EXERCISES

A. Using the information above, decide which use of *put in* is illustrated in each of the following examples:

1. Foreign workers are willing to put in 12-hour days and work weekends. _____
2. The aim is to put money in your pocket. _____
3. His boss told him to put in his request for a transfer. _____
4. The government plans to revise tax laws that were put in place in 1995. _____
5. He decided to put the new vice-president in charge of manufacturing. _____

B. Complete the sentences with the correct form of *put in*.

1. Think of what you could do if you .... a little effort.

2. Part of the new welfare-to-work program .... place last year.

3. Buyers tend to .... their orders at the end of the month.

4. Carole Jay has been .... charge of West Coast Operations.

5. He .... fewer than 100 hours a month at the office.

C. Discussion Questions

1. Do you have projects at work that require you to put in a lot of hours?

2. Is there anything that you would like to be put in charge of at your job? What would you not want to be put in charge of?

I should put in a bid

UNIT 35: Review
SPECIALIZE IN, SHUT DOWN, FIND OUT, PUT IN

A. **Select the phrasal verb that best completes the sentence:**

1. The bug causes the computer to freeze or ....
   (a) shot down   (b) shutting down   (c) shut down

2. W&L is a New York ad agency that .... marketing to kids and families.
   (a) specializing in (b) specializes in   (c) specializes on

3. As soon as we .... about the defect, we ordered a recall of the autos.
   (a) find out   (b) finding out   (c) found out

4. The executives .... a place a new growth strategy.
   (a) putting in   (b) puts in   (c) put in

5. I .... the hard way that stocks can go down as well as up.
   (a) find out   (b) found out   (c) finding out

B. **Rewrite the sentences by replacing the underlined word or phrase with the correct form of the appropriate phrasal verb:**

1. PTG are taking steps to ban Inter-TV, an interactive-television venture.
2. Investigators are trying to discover whether company officials destroyed documents.
3. In 1995, the copper-mining operation closed, taking many businesses with it.
4. RubberCo has established a plan to add 30 new employees in entry-level management positions.
5. GM has placed Ford in a difficult position.

C. **Find the errors in these sentences. There is one error in each sentence:**

1. A Texas attorney who specialize in the Freedom of Information Act released a series of confidential IRS memos.
2. The furnace was shutted down for two days for annual maintenance.
3. Grear is a partner at S&G, a firm specializes in patent law.
4. The company was forced to shutting down its music-sharing website.
5. Finding out if other franchisees are making money.

Unit 36:TAKE ON something/someone

STUDY THESE SENTENCES

In my new job I will have to **take on** additional responsibilities.	1	carry/accept a job/responsibility
The producer **took** him **on** as an assistant director.	2	employ someone
Thanks to the California-based company, special effects have **taken on** a whole new dimension.	3	adopt, develop an appearance/quality
Some new start-up companies are ready to **take on** the traditional telephone companies.	4	compete with

EXERCISES

A. Using the information above, decide which use of *take on* is illustrated in each of the following examples. Write the number on the line:

1. The computer manufacturer plans to take on Toshiba.   _____
2. The legal assistants took on much of the workload in preparing the case.   _____
3. When his company grew in size, he took on a partner.   _____
4. The latest tax laws have taken on a new level of complexity.   _____
5. The news channel designed to take on CNN hasn't had much success.   _____

B. Complete the sentences with a suitable form of *take on* (e.g., *is taking on*) and one of the words/phrases from the box. Be sure to use the correct article (e.g. a/the) with the noun where required:

bankrupt	work	investors	project	executive role

1. Ed Cox has .... at the firm.
2. We are so busy that we cannot .... any more .... right now.
3. When Stevens ...., he didn't know how hard it would be.
4. The company went .... after .... too much debt.
5. .... too much risk is a common problem for ....

C. Rewrite the sentences by replacing the underlined word or phrase with the correct form of *take on* (e.g. *is taking on*).

1. The author <u>was hired</u> by Knopf, a major American publisher.
2. The animal rights campaigner <u>has advocated against</u> some of the biggest US firms.
3. Netscape tried to <u>compete against</u> Microsoft with its web-browser.
4. As managers <u>assume</u> more and more responsibilities, they have less time to encourage and inspire their subordinates.

Unit 37: FILE FOR something

STUDY THESE SENTENCES

The Canadian company **filed for** bankruptcy last month.

1   **submit an official request**

The chairman's wife **filed for** divorce.

EXERCISES

A. Complete the sentences with a suitable form of *file for* (e.g., *is filing for*) and one of the words from the box. Be sure to use the correct article (e.g. a/the) with the noun where required:

drug company	tax refund	bankruptcy	airline	patent

1. She .... for the year 2005.
2. We plan to .... for the new device.
3. .... FDA approval for its anti-wrinkle cream.
4. .... reorganization under Chapter 11 last March.
5. Ten years ago, he .... personal ....

B. Review your answers for exercise A. Note the words that collocate with *file for* and write them on the lines below. The first one has been done for you.

File for a tax refund

....

....

....

....

....

....

C. Discussion: Finding information

1. How can you find out if a company has filed for bankruptcy?
2. Where does one file for a patent on a new product?
3. What is the procedure a company must follow in order to file for FDA approval?

Unit 38: PUT ON something; PUT something ON

STUDY THESE SENTENCES

PATTERNS: BE PUT ON something; PUT something ON something

I **put** a couple of handouts **on** the table.	1	place something on a concrete object
We want to be able to **put** the test **on** the web.	2	place something on an abstract object
She quickly **put on** her coat and ran out the door.	3	put clothes on your body/add makeup to the face

IDIOMS

The company was **put on** the market at $12 million.	4	**put on the market** =sell
He **put** his career **on hold** and headed to Alaska.	5	**put** something/someone **on hold** =postpone something for a time
Can I put you on hold?		=wait on the telephone

EXERCISES

A. **Using the information above, decide which use of *put on* is illustrated in each of the following examples. Write the number on the line:**

1. Many IPOs have been put on hold because of the downturn in the market. _____
2. They were put on a plane back to Malaysia. _____
3. New applicants are put on a waiting list. _____
4. The company would be put on the auction block in an effort to raise money.

_____

B. **Complete the sentences with the correct form of the verb *put* and the particle *on*. If there is one blank space, write the verb form together with the particle in that space.**

1. Plans to start the new project will be _____ hold until the New Year.
2. The government is _____ pressure _____ the university system to increase enrollments.
3. Italians _____ about $700 million _____ their credit cards each year.
4. *Can you _____ the sales meeting _____ your schedule?*
5. A local law _____ limits _____ rents for poor people.

C. Complete the sentences with a suitable form of *put on* (e.g., *is putting on*) and one of the words from the box. Be sure to use the correct article (e.g. *a/the*) with the noun where required:

bottom line	market	customers	flight	HR manager

1. .... him .... the short list for the job.

2. We can .... you .... the waiting list for ....

3. We don't want .... to be .... hold for more than 2 minutes.

4. The company was .... at $12 million.

5. The product .... millions .... the company's ....

D. Discussion

1. According to real estate trends, would now be a good time to put a house on the market?

2. Name a situation in which you might be *put on a waiting list*.

3. Fill in the blank: *I would put my career on hold if I had the opportunity to* ....

56

Unit 39: GO THROUGH something

STUDY THESE SENTENCES

The company is **going through** one of its toughest times in memory.

1 **undergo or experience** something (usually unpleasant)

The company expects the deal to **go through**.

2 **succeed**
agreements and laws go through

He **went through** his father's papers.

3 **sort out/organize**

We **go through** a lot of coffee.

4 **use, eat**

IDIOM
Real estate prices are about to **go through the roof**.

5 **go through the roof**
=increase (dramatically)

RELATED PHRASAL VERB
Julie decided that she just wasn't ready to **go through with** a career change.

6 **go through with** something
=proceed with something (usually difficult)

EXERCISES

A. **Using the information above, decide which use of *go through* is illustrated in each of the following examples:**

1. He wants to sit down and go through the figures with us. _____
2. The price of oil futures has gone through the roof. _____
3. I went through ten different contractors on this job. _____
4. All companies are going through the same problems. _____
5. He may leave the company if the reorganization plan goes through. _____

B. **Study the patterns below then add to the lists. Some examples have been provided:**

1. go through X (usually something negative)
   a divorce
   ....
   ....
   ....

2. X go through the roof
   prices
   ....
   ....
   ....

57

3. go through X

papers

----

4. go through with X

a lawsuit

C. Complete the sentences with a suitable form of *go through* (e.g., *is going through*) and one of the words from the box. Be sure to use the correct article (e.g. *a/the*) with the noun where required:

cost cutting	interest rates	tough period	deal	attorneys

1. Many companies have .... and come out stronger.
2. The government raised .... to stop inflation from .... the roof.
3. The management will be looking at .... once the merger ....
4. CAG's .... with Holden .... a year ago.
5. We .... three .... on this case before we finally settled it.

D. Discussion Questions

1. What type of training did you go through for your job?

I hope our proposal goes through

Unit 40: REVIEW
TAKE ON, FILE FOR, PUT ON, GO THROUGH

A. Select the phrasal verb that best completes the sentence:

1. The company decided not to .... the trade union over pensions and other benefits.
   (a) took on   (b) taking on   (c) take on

2. The Advanced Medical Systems unit has been .... sale.
   (a) putting on   (b) putted on   (c) put on

3. The designer house .... the market at $2 million.
   (a) was putting on   (b) was put on   (c) is put on

4. *I'd say the odds of the deal* .... *are 50:50.*
   (a) go through   (b) went through   (c) going through

5. Spectra .... for Chapter 11 bankruptcy protection last June.
   (a) filed for   (b) file for   (c) is filing for

B. Rewrite the sentences by replacing the underlined word or phrase with the correct form of the appropriate phrasal verb. Use a dictionary, if necessary:

1. Do you want to <u>scan</u> the list?
2. You don't know what I am <u>enduring</u> at work. It's very stressful.
3. I have been away and now I am <u>perusing</u> my email.
4. There are rumors that the mortgage lender may <u>claim</u> bankruptcy.
5. Let me <u>review</u> what we have done up to this point.
6. The organization is <u>experiencing</u> a difficult time.
7. Chairman Bill Mortimer has <u>accepted</u> the additional title of CEO.
8. Generic drugs have to <u>undergo</u> an approval process before they can be put on the market
9. The company is determined to <u>proceed</u> with the ROC merger.
10. Is there a process I can <u>follow</u> to help me decided whether to go or stay?

C. Match the beginning of each sentence with the most appropriate ending:

1. After 20 minutes on hold,   boom and bust in the 80s.
2. Houston went through   more business.
3. I wish you would put bagels   to limit its exposure to legal suits.
4. We are gearing up to take on   I finally got through to customer service.
5. DCI has filed for Chapter 11   on the menu.

CorpusLab Exercises 4

1. Phrasal Verbs based on ON
Fill in the blank with the appropriate form of *take, work, go, put, or rely*.

1. The ad company .... on a pro-smoking campaign for Philip Morris.
2. These days many people .... on to second careers.
3. Ed Cox has .... on an executive role at the firm.
4. The Korean market is so small that electronics companies .... on exports.
5. BA .... on hold a plan to buy 50 commuter planes.
6. Initially, the venture will .... on the parent company for financial support.
7. We are gearing up to .... on more business.
8. The designer house was .... on the market at $2 million.
9. Peter has .... on the strategic planning committee for a year.
10. The chairman .... on to say that the outlook was bright,

2. One phrasal verb fits all the sentences. Which is it?

I suggested we get together to .... the contract in some detail.
Carla .... her sales pitch, which was excellent.
They'd better not .... with their plans to cut our payments.
Tony .... a number of jobs before going into pharmaceuticals.
We'll lose the financing if the deal doesn't .... by next week,.
Do you want to .... the agenda?

Phrasal verb ....

3. Give the missing collocations in the following sentences

1. The company ran up large debts and had to file for ....
2, Susan was put in .... of the East Coast office.
3, The director is on another line. Can I put you on .... ?.
4. Our house was put on the .... at $350,000
5. The credit card company put in .... a series of measure to combat fraud.
6. Trouble in the Middle East caused the price of oil to go through the ....

4. PUT IN

1.	Buyers tend to put in their orders at the end of the month.
2.	Foreign workers are willing to put in 12-hour days.
3.	Think what you could do if you put in a little effort.
4.	Is it to late to put in a proposal?
5.	Email will be unavailable while we put in a new computer network
6.	.I put ten grand in that scheme.
7.	We need to put in a back-up power supply.

Assign each sentence to the appropriate meaning:

    A. **spend time/energy**   Sentences ....

    B. **submit/enter something**: Sentences ....

    C. **install**:   Sentences ....

5. Concordance for PUT ON

Look at the following concordance lines.

> ket. We don't want customers to be **put on** hold for more than 2 minutes. The

> aiting list. The designer house was **put on** the market at $2 million. Can you p

> ket at $2 million. Can you **put the sales meeting on** your schedule?. We should

> of candidates. The HR manager **put him on** the short list for the job. We can

> gels on the menu. The product **put millions on** the company's bottom line. The

> processor. If you want to **put lots of applications on** a PDA, buy this one. If yo

> problem, Vince. I will certainly **put you on** the programme on the following

> ary purposes. Your name has been **put on** the list and you will be notified onc

> at a few anxious customers **put long-term deals on** hold last week. Says that o

> ers > need > a drink of water, I **put the cup on** the counter and there's my extr

> rge of that. Okay? He has to **put the pressure on** the credit guys to get the cre

> ely to reverse state efforts to **put the brakes on** deregulation. PG&E'S PLAN'

> y." Each new market entrant **put the squeeze on** Enron's margins. What happe

113 matches	Original text order	Strings matching: put% @ on

1. Some of the uses of *put* are passive. Underline two of them.
2. There are two examples of the idiom *put on hold*. What is the setting for the use in the first concordance line?
3. The active uses of *put* have the form **put X on Y**. One of the concordance lines refers to a physical action of putting of one object on another. Which line is it?
4. The other uses of **put X on Y** are more abstract. List three of then.

    put .... on ....

    put .... on ....

    put .... on ....

Unit 41: GO INTO something

STUDY THESE SENTENCES

I **go into** the office at about 10 a.m.	1	**enter a location**
He decided to **go into** interior design.	2	**enter a particular job, profession, business**
He refused to **go into** detail about his expansion plans.	3	**describe, talk about** a topic
A lot of work **went into** the planning stage.	4	**time/money/effort put into something**
Sales diminished and the retailer **went into** liquidation.	5	**enter a state**

IDIOMS

The new rules go into effect in 2010.	6	**go into effect** = new rules/laws, etc. officially begin
The airline industry **went into** recession after 9/11.	7	**go into recession/go into debt,** etc.

EXERCISES

A. Using the information above, decide which use of *go into* is illustrated in each of the following examples:

1. He went into business six years ago with 4000 rubles. _____
2. Every day I watched the office workers go into the building. _____
3. Most of the money went into small cap and emerging market funds. _____
4. The new car tax went into effect in 1998. _____
5. The talks must avoid going into too much detail. _____

B. Create full sentences with an appropriate form of *go into* using the words provided in the brackets. The first one has been done for you.

1. (Clare/journalism)
Clare went into journalism.
2. (mine/production/1997)

....

3. (leased planes/service/next month)

....

4. (since/the early eighties/billions of dollars/research on heart disease)

....

5. (report on pensions/great detail/on the problems/facing many people)

....

Unit 42: FIGURE OUT something

STUDY THESE SENTENCES

OTHER PATTERNS figure someone out, figure out what/that ....

I still haven't **figured out** all the rules.   1 **understand, work out**
                                                                find out

The engineers are trying to **figure out** what
happened.

EXERCISES

A. Complete the sentences with a suitable form of *figure out* (e.g., *is figuring out*) and
one of the words from the box. Be sure to use the correct article (e.g. *a/the*) with the
noun where required:

solution	tax	services	money	customers

1. We owe it to our .... how we can do a better job.
2. Nobody could .... where .... was going.
3. It doesn't take a rocket scientist to ....
4. We've got to .... ways to expand .... we provide.
5. We're .... how much .... we owe.

B. Draw a line between the two halves of each sentence. There is more than one correct
answer for each. How many different combinations can you make?

1. I am sure Sandy can figure   out why my computer keeps crashing.
2. I'm trying to figure out   that being famous has its drawbacks.
3. Some companies have figured out   what the economy will be like next year.
4. It didn't take me long to figure   out a way to do it.
5. Everyone is trying to figure   out how to avoid paying state taxes.

C. Study the patterns below then add to the lists:

(a) figure out X   (b) figure out what X...
a solution   happened

....
....

Unit 43: FOCUS ON something

STUDY THESE SENTENCES

The ad campaign **focused on** young consumers.

*We must always **focus on** what the clients want.*

1   **pay attention to one thing**

EXERCISES

A. Complete the sentences with a suitable form of focus on (e.g., is focusing on) and one of the words from the box. Be sure to use the correct article (e.g. a/the) with the noun where required:

warehouse	results	company	price	acquisitions

  1. Guy Berne says he plans to ....as way to grow the business.
  2. She .... improving inventory control in ....
  3. We can improve .... by .... inventory management.
  4. The retailer decided to .... quality rather than ....
  5. At this ...., we .... results.

B. Correct the errors in these sentences. There is one error in each:

  1. We're in it for the long haul and we focusing on the big picture.
  2. The government is now focus on cutting its debt.
  3. Sprint has decide to focus on a series of new wireless products.
  4. The company focusing on long-term brand development.
  5. The new executive was brought in to focus day-to-day operations.

C. Discussion Questions

1. What does it mean to *focus on the big picture*?

2. In your opinion, what is most important for a company to focus on: quality, price or customer satisfaction?

I 'm going to focus on mergers and acquisitions

Unit 44: GET OUT of something; GET something OUT

STUDY THESE SENTENCES

OTHER PATTERNS: get out of (doing) something

*Sorry I'm late. I couldn't **get out** of the office.*	**1**	leave a building or place or situation
Do you think you can **get out** all the Americans who need to be evacuated?	**2**	remove someone/something from a place/situation
Can you **get** your dictionary **out**?	**3**	remove from a bag, etc. *similar to take out*

IDIOMS

I can't believe that you're trying to **get out of** finishing that job.	**4**	**get out of doing** something = avoid doing something
He is looking for a way to **get out** of the deal.	**5**	**get out of the deal/agreement**

EXERCISES

A. Using the information above, decide which use of *get out* is illustrated in each of the following examples. Write the number on the line:

1. He's trying to get out of doing that job. _____
2. On weekends I like to get out of town. _____
3. *Get me out of here.* _____
4. She now wants to get out of her new contract. _____
5. Getting oil out of the ground is never easy. _____

B. Complete the sentences with the correct form of *get out*. If there are two blank spaces, put the particle in the second space.

1. The board wants to _____ results _____ faster.
2. He started a business a year after _____ of college.
3. We felt it was time to _____ of manufacturing and focus on services.
4. I called you as soon as I _____ of my meeting.
5. We have to _____ the impurities _____ of the water.

C. Investigate these uses of *get out*. Use a dictionary to help you, if necessary. What do the meanings imply in a business sense? Explain in your own words.

1. If you can't stand the heat, you should **get out of the kitchen**.
2. He needs to **get his head out of the clouds**.
3. I hope we can **get** something positive **out** of the meeting.

Unit 45: REVIEW
GO INTO, FIGURE OUT, FOCUS ON, GET OUT

A. Select the phrasal verb that best completes the sentence:

1. Ms. Stern believes the US economy is .... a recession now, but could pull out of it by the end of the year.
   (a) goes into   (b) going into   (c) go into
2. People have trouble .... their tax bill.
   (a) figures out   (b) figured out   (c) figuring out
3. When the new law .... effect, smoking will be banned in restaurants.
   (a) goes into   (b) go into   (c) going into
4. BDG is .... of the electronics business.
   (a) got out   (b) goes out   (c) getting out
5. Instead of being in the office all day, he wants to .... and meet clients.
   (a) gets out   (b) get out   (c) getting out

B. Rewrite the sentences by replacing the underlined word or phrase with the correct form of the appropriate phrasal verb:

1. A new GM car has been designed and will <u>enter</u> production in two years.
2. He managed to <u>learn</u> how the technology could help his business.
3. Bill quit the university to <u>join</u> the family business.
4. The new guidelines will not <u>take effect</u> until next year.
5. ABC Worldwide has <u>joined</u> partnership with ICL plc.

C. Match the beginning of each sentence with the most appropriate ending. There is one answer for each:

1. We went into this business	into a recession with these kinds of loan problems.
2. After 15 years,	I wanted to get out of sales.
3. The executive team is	focused on the company's core business.
4. About $400 million of debt could	go into default
5. We may go	because of the high growth potential.
6. Wayne Curtis was a machine technician	says she plans to go into business with her husband.
7. Connie Chung	before going into management.
8. The auto manufacturer hasn't yet	figured out how to avoid a multibillion dollar tax bill.
9. Since leaving college,	before going into real estate.
10. Lisa went through a number of jobs	he has been focused on starting his own business.

Unit 46: GET INTO something

STUDY THESE SENTENCES

Some music fans tried to **get into** the concert without paying.	1	enter a place
You get paid a lot of money when you **get into** pro sports.	2	involve oneself in
She was hoping to **get into** Harvard.	3	join an organization
It's a good time to **get into** natural gas stocks.	4	buy/acquire/invest

IDIOMS

Martha Stewart was doing well, but then **she got into trouble** with the law.	5	**get into trouble** =get into a difficult situation
While he was in college, **he got into drugs.**	6	**get into** something =develop a habit/a routine

EXERCISES

A. Using the information above, decide which use of *get into* is illustrated in each of the following examples:

1. I'd like to get into consulting. _____
2. Some companies get into trouble after a period of rapid growth. _____
3. We need to get our products into more stores. _____
4. If you have bad grades, it is almost impossible to get into the top business schools. _____
5. The best way to get into foreign stocks is through mutual funds. _____

B. Complete the sentences with a suitable form of *get into* (e.g., *getting into*) and one of the words from the box. Be sure to use the correct article (e.g. *a/the*) with the noun where required:

late 80s and early 90s	inspectors	half-billion gallons	MBA program	interactive-game business

1. There was a report today saying that _____ North Korea as early as January.
2. The insurance company _____ trouble in _____.
3. An estimated _____ of oil _____ American waterways every year.
4. All the major studios are _____.
5. She was really hoping to _____.

68

Unit 47: TURN OUT

STUDY THESE SENTENCES

The Christmas sales season may **turn out to** be disappointing.	1	**happen, occur (unexpectedly), end up**
The plane maker hopes to **turn out** 10 new aircraft a month.	2	**turn out** something = produce
Four thousand workers **turned out** for the strike meeting.	3	**go to an event; attend a meeting**

EXERCISES

A. **Using the information above, decide which use of *turn out* is illustrated in each of the following examples:**

1. The plant is turning out 1 million DVD players a year. _____
2. All of the reps turned out for the monthly sales meeting. _____
3. Last year turned out to be a good one for bondholders. _____
4. November turned out to be the worst month for retail sales. _____
5. Workers at the factory were turning out brand name running shoes. _____

B. **Match the beginning of each sentence with the most appropriate ending:**

1. It seemed like a good idea at the time,
2. Racket manufacturers turn out
3. The photos for the new ad campaign
4. She said that oil stocks would rise
5. August turned out to be

a very strong month for exports.
turned out well.
and it turned out that she was right.
new models virtually every year.
but it turned out not to be.

C. **Complete the sentences with a suitable form of turn out (e.g., *is turning out*) and one of the words from the box. Be sure to use the correct article (e.g. *a/the*) with the noun where required:**

inherit	profits	beneficial	financing	company

1. .... did well, but not for long, as it ....
2. It .... that most millionaires didn't .... their money; they made it themselves.
3. The online bookstore isn't .... any .... yet.
4. The start-up's .... could .... to be inadequate.
5. Managed care has .... to be .... for drug companies.

Unit 48: GO BACK to somewhere/something

STUDY THESE SENTENCES

We're **going back** to California in June.	1	return (to a place)
The use of personal computers **goes back** to the eighties. Her career in show business **went back** to 1947.	2	date back (= the use of personal computers started in the eighties)
He **went back** to school to finish his degree. *I want to* **go back** *to something that John said.*	3	return (to a situation or topic or activity)

IDIOMS *We need to* **go back to square one.** *We need to* **go back to the drawing board.**	4	go back to square one = we need to start from the beginning

RELATED PHRASAL VERB **go back on** your word/promise/agreement	**go back on** =not do what you said you would do

EXERCISES

A. **Using the information above, decide which use of** *go back* **is illustrated in each of the following examples:**

1. Her involvement in the museum goes back 10 years. _____
2. His proposal was to go back to the previous voting system. _____
3. The software has some bugs and so we have to go back to the drawing board. _____
4. I went back to Houston and got a job in the oil industry. _____
5. We'll have to go back to the board for approval of the takeover bid. _____

B. Complete the sentences with a suitable form of *going back* (e.g., *is going back*) and one of the words from the box. Be sure to use the correct article (e.g. *a/the*) with the noun where required:

methods	airline	bank	sales	compete

1. Do you ever think of .... into .... ?
2. They have .... on their promise not to .... with us.
3. Some farmers are .... to traditional farming ....
4. Steve is .... to what he does best: running an ....
5. We can always .... to the .... and ask for more money.

C. Match the beginning of each sentence with the most suitable ending. Some may have more than one correct answer:

1. After the accident, we had every factory go   back into technology stocks.
2. I'd better go   back to the bank and ask for
                                                          more money.
3. Now is the time to go   back and review their safety
                                                          procedures.
4. Once the crisis is over, we can go   back to the office.
5. We can always go   back to business as usual.

D. Discussion Questions

1. If you had the opportunity to go back to school, would you? If yes, what subject or degree would you pursue and why? If not, why not?

2. If you were able to go back in time, is there anything in your career path that you would like to change?

Unit 49: COMPLY WITH something

STUDY THESE SENTENCES

The project failed to **comply with** federal clean-water regulations.

1   do what is required

EXERCISES

A. Fill in the blanks with the correct form of *comply with*:

1. Sykes said that GHF did not .... the terms of the contract.
2. I have to go to a workshop on .... anti-discrimination laws.
3. The spokeswoman said that the company will .... all consumer protection laws.
4. Mr. Rico said that the bank had .... all requirements under Swiss law.
5. The company admitted it had not been .... the conditions of the loan.

B. Choose an appropriate word from the box to best complete these sentences. Note the part of speech next to the word (e.g. noun, verb, adjective):

progress	advertise	steps	disciplinary	internal

1. The energy company has to release its ....emails to comply with the court order.

2. The CEO was accused of not taking reasonable .... to ensure that employees comply with the law.

3. The US has made some .... in complying with the agreement.

4. Drug companies can .... their products as long as they comply with FDA regulations.

5. Failure to comply with these regulations can result in .... action.

He's complying with the indoor smoking ban

Unit 50: REVIEW

GET INTO, TURN OUT, GO BACK, COMPLY WITH

A. Select the phrasal verb that best completes the sentence:

1. *I didn't know what I was* ....
(a) get into   (b) got into   (c) getting into

2. *Would you advise* .... *to school — for other small business owners?*
(a) go back   (b) going back   (c) gone back

3. *I applied to four universities and* .... *all of them.*
(a) got into   (b) get into   (c) getting into

4. *The suspicious package found in the mall* .... *to be a toaster.*
(a) turning out   (b) turn out   (c) turned out

5. *We're doing our best to* .... *what the committee is asking for.*
(a) comply with   (b) complying with   (c) complied with

6. *The root causes of the problem* .... *to the 80s.*
(a) goes back   (b) go back   (c) going back

7. *I've always wanted to* .... *real estate.*
(a) getting into   (b) gets into   (c) get into

8. *We hope the sale* .... *well.*
(a) turns out   (b) turning out   (c) turns on

9. *I know Heidi is not thrilled about* .... *to Dallas.*
(a) goes back   (b) gone back   (c) going back

10. *Banking* .... *to be not quite what I expected.*
(a) turned out   (b) turning out   (c) turn out

B. Answer yes or no to the following questions about the phrasal verbs:

1. If somebody says, *Time to go back to work,* is s/he returning to work?
2. If somebody says, *I hope I can get into Harvard Business School,* does s/he hope to be accepted?
3. If China was *successful in getting into the WTO,* does this mean they are now part of the WTO?
4. Somebody asks, *how do we get our products into more stores?* Does this mean s/he wants to sell more products?
5. If *we have to comply with FDA regulations,* then we do not have to do what is required. True?

CorpusLab Exercises 5

1. Phrasal Verbs based on OUT
Fill in the blank with the appropriate form of *find, point, figure, turn, or get*.

1. Last year _____ out to be a good one for investors.
2. I will _____ out more this upcoming week and let you know.
3. As soon as we _____ out about the defect, we ordered a product recall.
4. I should _____ out that not everyone agrees with this assessment.
5. She now wants to _____ out of her new contract.
6. Call me as soon as you _____ out of the meeting.
7. The auto manufacturer hasn't yet _____ out how to avoid a multibillion dollar tax bill.
8. The Christmas sales season is _____ out to be disappointing.
9. Can you _____ out how to stop my computer from crashing all the time?
10. They _____ out errors in the accounts

2. One phrasal verb fits all the sentences. Which is it?

How did Neron _____ this mess?
Some companies _____ trouble after a period of rapid growth.
If you download the file, a virus may _____ your computer.
She's hoping to _____ Stanford University.
I don't want to _____ the details of the case.

Phrasal verb _____

3. TURN OUT

1.	The suspicious package in the mail turned out to be a toaster.
2.	The factory is turning out 2,000 units a day.
3.	She said oil stocks would rise and it turns out she was right.
4.	The Business School turns out a hundred graduates a year.
5.	He's not sorry that things turned out the way they did.
6.	A lot of people turned out for the product launch.
7.	The deal turned out to be very profitable.

Assign each sentence to the appropriate meaning:
  A. **occur/happen/end up**   Sentences _____
  B. **attend something**:   Sentences _____
  C. **produce something**:   Sentences _____

4. Concordance for GO INTO

Look at the following concordance lines.

oblems. The new guidelines will not **go into** effect until next year. Ms. Stern belie
by the end of the year. He refused to **go into** detail about his expansion plans. Abo
on of debt could go into default. We **went into** this business because of the high gro
, the TV announcer, says she plans to **go into** business with her husband. A new GI
t through a number of jobs before **going into** real estate. The leased planes will go
ext month. Bill quit the university to **go into** the family business. I go into the offi
rsity to go into the family business. I **go into** the office at about 10am. The mine wo
 effect in 2010. ABC Worldwide has **gone into** partnership with ICL plc. Wayne Cu
before going into management. He **went into** business six years ago with 4000 rub
bles. In the downturn, many houses **went into** foreclosure. Sales diminished and th
e. Sales diminished and the retailer **went into** liquidation. Most of the money wen
to the stairwell and standby. Do not **go into** the stairwell. Further instructions wi
ts. The new contracts are expected to **go into** effect this year. "We used our purcha
sman Mark Palmer, who declined to **go into** further detail or discuss specific comp

53 matches	Original text order	Strings matching: (\bgo[eni]?[sne]?g?\b|went)\W+into\b

1. Some of the examples of *go into* are followed by an article or demonstrative pronoun. These examples involve entering a specific place or thing. Write down the verb and object.

    went into this business

    ....

    ....

    ....

2. There are two main idioms in the examples. One is *go into detail*. What is the other one?

    ....

3. The remaining uses have the form go into followed by the object describing an abstract state or condition. In these examples there is no article before the object. Write down the verb and object.

    go into business

    ....

    ....

    ....

Unit 51: KEEP UP (WITH) something

STUDY THESE SENTENCES

The search engine company was unable to **keep up with** Google.	1	**keep up with** =maintain, compete with, catch up with
The cellular phone makers could not **keep up with demand**.	2	**keep up with demand** =meet demand
Sales were so good that supply couldn't **keep up**.	3	**keep up** =continue

Related Phrasal Verb
I watch Bloomberg TV to **keep up on** the stock market.

keep up on
=stay informed about something

EXERCISES

A. Complete the sentences with the correct form of the verb *keep*. If there are two blank spaces in the sentence, write *up* in the second space:

1. My gym membership was too expensive to _____.
2. The state needs the sales tax to _____ revenue _____.
3. He's spending too much. If he _____ it _____, he'll soon be broke.
4. It is a daily battle for the Mom and Pop stores to _____ with the large chains.
5. *Do you* _____ *with any of your old colleagues?*

B. Complete the sentences with a suitable form of *keep up* (e.g., *is keeping up*) and one of the words or phrases from the box. Be sure to use the correct article (e.g. *a/the*) with the noun where required:

cost of living	progress	constant struggle	capacity	revenues

1. Their income is not _____ with _____.
2. If we can _____ the pace, _____ could double in the next three years.
3. It's _____ to _____ with the changing regulations.
4. We had to increase _____ to _____ with retail demand.
5. _____ *me* _____ *to date on your* _____.

76

Unit 52: GET BACK

STUDY THESE SENTENCES

PATTERNS get back to somewhere/something/someone, get something/someone back,
get back at

I'd love to **get back** to California, but I'm looking at other places as well.	1	return	
We are concerned about **getting** our investment **back**.	2	have something/someone again	
Our goal is to **get back** to business as usual.	3	return to an abstract place/activity	

IDIOMS

They're trying to **get back at Susan**.	4	**get back at** = take revenge	
Sorry it has taken me so long to **get back to** you.	5	**get back to someone** =contact somebody at a later date), **get in touch with**	
We're hoping the expansion program will **get back** on track.	6	**get back on track** =return to a previous state, usually for the better	

EXERCISES

A. Read the following sentences. Group those which have a similar meaning and rewrite them under the appropriate heading. There are two correct choices for each heading.

(a) The company needs to get back on the path to healthy growth.
(b) Bmart said its challenge would be in getting customers back.
(c) When did you get back from vacation?
(d) He will return from vacation and get back to work.
(e) It's good to see your career is getting back on track.
(f) Please get any comments back to me by tomorrow.
(g) He wanted to get back to the office as soon as possible.
(h) Let's get back to business.

get back/return to a place

get something/someone back again

get back/return to an abstract place/activity

get back/return to a previous state, usually for the better

B. Complete the sentences with the correct form of *get* and the particle *back*. If there is one blank space, write the verb form together with the particle in that space.

1. We sent him numerous letters, but he never _____ to us.
2. The important thing is to _____ the company _____ to profitability.
3. I will raise that concern with her and make sure she _____ to you.
4. Please _____ any comments _____ to me by tomorrow
5. He's been out sick and only _____ in the office today.

C. Rewrite the sentences below by replacing the underlined words in each sentence with an appropriate use of *get back*. Make other adjustments to the sentence where necessary, so that it makes sense.

1. If you could <u>call me</u> as soon as you can, I'd really appreciate it.
2. When Heather <u>arrives</u>, she'll be able to get the information.
3. He was anxious <u>to become involved in the hair care business once again.</u>
4. I'll <u>contact you again</u> with a plan on how to do this.
5. The goal is to <u>return</u> to 20% gross profit margins

D. Discussion Question

Your colleague is discouraged because s/he was recently laid off his job. How could you help him/her to get back on the right track? What suggestions would you offer?

Unit 53: CONTRACT OUT something

STUDY THESE SENTENCES

OrangeJet **contracts out** virtually all of its repairs.

1   hire an outside person/contractor to do something

EXERCISES

A. Complete the sentences with a suitable form of *contract out* (e.g., *is contracting out*) and one of the words or phrases from the box. Be sure to use the correct article (e.g. *a/the*) with the noun where required:

tasks	specialists	trend	outsourcing

1. Banks are increasingly .... IT services .... to ....
2. .... involves .... to companies those services that are not essential to the core business.
3. .... among manufacturers is to .... for legal work, cleaning services and catering.
4. American Motors plans to .... more non-assembly ....

B. Correct the error in each sentence. There is one error in each.

1. Manufacturing of the products is contract out to keep capital and inventory costs

2. Last May, VVX contracts the job out to Teasewell Services.

3. Airlines may contract in services currently provided in-house, such as maintenance and ticket sales.

4. Communications technology allows companies to contracting out most support functions while maintaining the core business in-house.

I see they have contracted out security

C. Discussion

1. Does your company contract out any of its work? Discuss the pros and cons of contracting out.

Unit 54: COME OUT

STUDY THESE SENTENCES

OTHER PATTERNS: come out of somewhere, come out that ...

He **came out** of the elevator with a couple of friends.	1	**leave (a place, a position)**
On May 1st we **came out** with a new home equity product.	2	**release, make public (reports/info/feelings, etc.)**
Hope you will ***come out*** *and support the team.*	3	**publicly show support for/against something**
The net cash flow **came out to be** $1.2 million a day.	4	**come out to be** =equals

IDIOMS

The firm that offers superior service at the same price always **comes out ahead**.	5	**come out ahead** = have an advantage
It's impossible to say which of the two companies will **come out on top**.	6	**come out on top** = be successful; win

EXERCISES

A. Using the information above, decide which use of *come out* is illustrated in each of the following examples:

1. Do you know if they have come out with a formal proposal? _____
2. In our battle with ERC, we need to come out on top. _____
3. The special dividend comes out to about $5 billion in cash. _____
4. The chairman came out against the decision. _____
5. Dwyer will come out of retirement to become chairman of the company.
   _____

B. Complete the sentences with a suitable form of *come out* (e.g., *is coming out*) and one of the words from the box. Be sure to use the correct article (e.g. *a/the*) with the noun where required:

plan	sales reports	resign	software	ex-CEO

1. The story .... that the CEO had threatened to ....
2. .... of the company had to .... of retirement.

81

3. We were surprised by .... that .... today.
4. The chairman of the board .... squarely against ....
5. A new release of .... will .... in July.

C. Study the patterns below then add to the lists. Use a dictionary, if necessary.

(a) come out of X	(b) come out with X	(c) X came out
a slump	a series of books	the story
....	....	....
....	....	....
....	....	....

D. Discussion Questions

1. Describe a situation where you or someone you know really came out on top.

2. Do you think it is common for a person to come out of retirement? Can you think of a person (famous or not) who has come out of retirement? In your opinion, was this a wise decision for that person to make?

Unit 55 REVIEW
KEEP UP, GET BACK, CONTRACT OUT, COME OUT

A. Select the phrasal verb that best completes the sentence:

1. It _____ that the politician had received money from the oil company.
(a) comes out   (b) coming out   (c) came out

2. The company is trying to remedy the downside of _____ the work _____.
   (a) contracts ____ out   (b) contracting ____ out (c) contracted ____ out

3. I _____ to getting back there to watch a UT game with you.
(a) looking forward   (b) looks forward   (c) look forward

4. *Thanks for _____ to me.*
(a) getting back   (b) got back   (c) get back

5. I try to _____ with the new technology.
(a) keeps up   (b) keeping up   (c) keep up

B. Rewrite the sentences by replacing the underlined word or phrase with the correct form of the appropriate phrasal verb:

1. The shares fell as more information <u>was released</u> about the company's debt problem.
2. *I'll start on this when I <u>return</u>.*
3. *We have not <u>devised</u> an alternative schedule yet*
4. The truth will <u>be known</u> in the end.
5. To stay profitable, we have to <u>meet</u> consumer demands.

C. Read the sentence, then circle yes/no in answer to the question that follows:

1. The senator came out against the Republican party resolution. Was the senator in favor of the resolution? yes/no
2. There is no guarantee that good managers will come out on top. This means there is no guarantee that the managers will succeed. yes/no
3. *If you could get back with me today, that would be great.* This person does not want you to call him/her today. yes/no
4. *Let's see what comes out of the strategic review.* This means let's wait for a reaction to the review. yes/no
5. The value per share comes out to $5.25. This means the value of each share is more than $5.25. yes/no

Unit 56: BRING IN

STUDY THESE SENTENCES

The new franchise tax **brings in** $1 billion a year.	1	earn, make money
Harvey **brought in** new management, but the unit never performed up to expectations.	2	bring in someone – get help from a person with particular skills or characteristics
The retailer is updating its stores to **bring in** new customers.	3	bring in customers, attract people

EXERCISES

A. Using the information above, decide which use of *bring in* is illustrated in each of the following examples:

1. The CIO brought in Maldonado to install an automated sales tracking system.

2. Donald Trump expected the new casino to **bring in** revenue of $600 million a year.
   _____

3. The takeover will give a boost to the PR company and bring in several blue-chip clients.
   _____

B. Complete the sentences with a suitable form of *bring in* (e.g., *bringing in*) and one of the words from the box. Be sure to use the correct article (e.g. *a/the*) with the noun where required:

cost-cutter	investors	successful promotion	new CEO	revenue

1. In order to grow her company, Ms. Clements decided to ....outside ....'

2. Last quarter, the chairman .... a well-known .... to improve the bank's financial controls.

3. .... a flood of new customers.

4. The company aims to .... half its .... from outside the US.

5. .... is probably going to .... new people.

C. Discussion Questions

1. Explain whether you agree/disagree with the following statement: *Advertising is the only way to bring in customers.*

2. Describe a situation in which your company/a company might bring in somebody.

Unit 57: PAY OFF

STUDY THESE SENTENCES

Tom Murphy is confident that his expansion plans will **pay off**.

1   result in success, have good consequence

Idioms
Paying off customs officials is a normal cost of business in some countries.

2   pay off someone/pay someone off =offer money to someone to do something, usually illegal

I use my credit a lot, but **pay** it **off** every month.

3   pay off something/pay something off (e.g., a debt)

EXERCISES

A. Using the information above, decide which use of *pay off* is illustrated in each of the following examples:

1. More people are struggling to pay off their credit card balances each month.

                                                _____

2. He is accused of paying off police officers to avoid a criminal investigation.

                                                _____

3. The auto marketing campaign to attract young professionals is paying off.

                                                _____

B. Complete the sentences with the correct form *pay off*:

1. Using aluminum is costlier, but it _____ because it is easier to install and costs less to maintain.
2. Many consumers are finding it difficult to _____ their credit card debts.
3. Sales are increasing, indicating that the investment in new technology is starting to _____.
4. The start-up company will put aside some money to _____ investors.
5. The company's global growth strategy is _____, with strong worldwide sales of light trucks making up for weaker demand in the US.

C. Discussion Questions

1. Describe a situation in which you invested a lot of time or money and it really paid off.
2. What advice would you have for somebody who has difficulty paying off their credit cards each month?
3. Do you agree or disagree with this statement: It pays off to continuously update your professional skills through continuing education. Have you experienced this kind of pay off in your career?

Unit 58: LAY OFF

STUDY THESE SENTENCES

The computer maker will **lay off** another 5%   1   fire - let go
of its workforce.

EXERCISES

A. **Complete the sentences with the correct form** *lay off*:

1. Factories are shutting production lines and .... workers because of reduced demand for their products.
2. Carla Smith was .... last December, but got a new job 3 months later.
3. Lenoco had to .... 10% of its workforce last year.
4. As part of a restructuring package, the company .... 25% of its workforce.
5. The company says it plans to .... 2,500 people at a cost of $200 million.

B. **Complete the sentences with a suitable form of** *lay off* **and one of the words from the box. Be sure to use the correct article (e.g.** *a/the*) **with the noun where required:**

cash flow	fashion chain	temporary	automated software systems	downsizing

1. .... closed eight stores and .... 300 employees.
2. Since being .... , she has worked in a series of .... jobs.
3. As phone companies merge, they may .... more operators and replace them with ....
4. The company owner had some problems with .... , forcing her to .... three people last year.
5. We want to avoid .... and .... people ....

C. **Discussion Questions**

1. How do you react when you hear in the media that a large company has laid off hundreds of workers?

2. What advice would you have for a friend who was just laid off?

Unit 59: BRING OUT

STUDY THESE SENTENCES

The auto maker **brought out** a line of popular minivans in the 90s.

1   bring out something/bring something out (e.g., a product)

Idiom
We strive to **bring out the best** in our employees.

2   bring out the best/worst in X = make more noticeable

EXERCISES

A. Match the beginning of each sentence with the most suitable ending:

1. Waiters
2. Sales
3. Long flights
4. A good boss
5. The auction

should bring out the bargain hunters
in overcrowded planes bring out the worst in people.
knows how to bring out the best in people.
brought out the champagne.
are a good way to bring out the crowds.

B. Complete the sentences with a suitable form of *bring out* (e.g., *is bringing out*) and one of the words from the box. Be sure to use the correct article (e.g. *a/the*) with the noun where required:

poverty	settlement	new chip	publishers	competitors

1. Intel plans to .... next year.
2. You can't wait for someone to .... you .... of ....
3. Many .... have .... encyclopedias on CDROM.
4. We reached .... to .... the company .... of bankruptcy.
5. ADG is far behind its .... in .... new products.

C. Discussion Questions

1. Is it a boss' duty to bring out the best in his/her employees? What sorts of things can a boss do to motivate employees in a positive way? Talk about your experience as a boss and/or employee.

Unit 60: REVIEW
BRING IN, PAY OFF, LAY OFF, BRING OUT

A. Rewrite the sentences by replacing the underlined word or phrase with the correct form of the appropriate phrasal verb:

1. The new Madonna album <u>earned</u> $25 million in its first week.
2. The auto maker has often been slow in <u>releasing</u> new models.
3. They cut down on spending and started to <u>clear</u> their debts.
4. The CIO <u>hired</u> Maldonado to install an automated sales tracking system.
5. After being <u>let go</u> from three companies, he decided to become an entrepreneur and set up his own company.
6. It is not clear whether a long-term strategy based on aggressive growth will <u>be worth it</u>.

B. Find the errors in these sentences. There is one error in each sentence:

1. I've got all the paperwork at home, I'll bring in tomorrow.
2. Prodigal is laying 250 workers and hiring an outside company to take over its customer service operations.
3. The new CEO is probably going to bringing in new people.
4. We had delays bring products out last year, but we are moving ahead now.
5. The takeover will give a boost to the PR company and brought in several blue-chip clients.
6. These days traveling by air seems to bring in the worst in people.

I am afraid we were a bit late bringing this out

CorpusLab Exercises 6

1. Phrasal Verbs based on COME
Fill in the blank with _in, out from_ or _up_ to make the appropriate phrasal verb.

1. Enron said it's working with lenders to come _____ with an acceptable agreement on the debt.
2. The accounting firm came _____ for a lot of criticism.
3. Natural gas imports to the US mostly come _____ Canada.
4. The renovations at Owen Field are well ahead of schedule and will come _____ under budget.
5. On May 1st we came _____ with a new home equity product.
6. The average cost came _____ to be $6.25.
7. I asked one of our analysts to take a look, but so far he's come _____ empty.
8. Can you check to see if you have come _____ with any pricing on those winter deals we discussed last week?
9. _There's loads more where this came _____!_
10. Let's see what comes _____ of the energy review

2. Phrasal Verbs based on GO
Fill in the blank with _back, on, through_ or _into_ to make the appropriate phrasal verb.

1. I'd like to know what's going _____ in the DealBench team
2. The new policy is expected to go _____ effect next year.
3. We're going _____ the process of settling claims.
4. What's going _____ at Enron?
5. I figure this is my only opportunity to go _____ to school.
6. plant in Sardinia went _____ full commercial operation in December 2000
7. Your continued efforts are critical to the company as we go _____ this decision making process.
8 Microsoft announced that the newest Xbox will go _____ sale Nov 8.
9. The electricity rate will go _____ effect next month
10. The company is going _____ hard times and faces a merger with Dynegy.

3. One phrasal verb fits all the sentences. Which is it?

_Thanks--and _____ the good work._
My gym membership was too expensive to _____
The company is adding staff to _____ with demand.
It's difficult to _____ with all the Health and Safety regulations.
We will have to double our network capacity to _____ with usage.
I try to _____ with new developments in manufacturing.

Phrasal verb _____

4. Give the missing collocations in the following sentences

1. Now that the labor dispute is over, we aim to get back to .... as usual.
2, In the battle for market share, we need to make sure we come out on ....
3, The work environment is designed to bring out the .... in our employees.
4. I want to bring someone in to get our overseas expansion program back on ....
5. ADG plans to lay off 20% of its ....

5. BRING IN

1.	The executive was brought in to oversee franchising.
2.	The rise in sales tax will bring in an extra $2.5 million.
3.	We will bring in consultants to handle the restructuring.
4.	ABG is updating its image to bring in younger customers.
5.	I was brought in to run the marketing department.
6.	Our national campaign is bringing in new clients every day.

Assign each sentence to the appropriate meaning:

A. **receive money**   Sentences ....

B. **recruit/hire someone:**   Sentences ....

C. **attract people to a place:**   Sentences ....

6. One phrasal verb fits all the sentences. Which is it?

If you could .... to me as soon as possible, I would greatly appreciate it.

We've got to .... to work on that.

I'll check those dates and .... to you.

I'd love to .... to California.

We're hoping the expansion program will ....on track.

Phrasal verb ....

Unit 61: CUT BACK (ON) something

STUDY THESE SENTENCES

We'll have to **cut back** our spending for a bit.

    1   reduce, limit

Hotels are **cutting back on** the number of front-desk employees.

EXERCISES

A. Match the beginning of the sentence with the most appropriate ending:

1. Unitel closed one office in Chicago and cut
2. Manufacturers are working hard to cut
3. The discount airline cut

4. Higher interest rates will cut
5. The apparel industry continued to cut

back consumer spending.
back its flight schedule by 20%.
back on inventories to reduce
   financing costs.
back excess inventories.
back staff in the New York office.

B. Complete the sentences with a suitable form of cut back (e.g., is cutting back) and one of the words from the box. Be sure to use the correct article (e.g. a/the) with the noun where required:

respondents	home builders	DVD drives	purchase	slowdown

1. The Air Force .... its planned .... of smart weapons.
2. Memory chip buyers .... their orders because of .... in the laptop computer market.
3.. .... in California .... sharply on new construction in October.
4. Computer manufacturers are expected to .... on orders of microprocessors and ....
5. Less than 40% of .... say that they .... on driving, even occasionally, for environmental reasons.

C. Discussion Questions

1. What does it mean when a company makes cut-backs?

2. When consumers cut back on spending, what sorts of things do they usually stop buying?

Unit 62: HEAD UP something

STUDY THESE SENTENCES

Mary **heads up** the firm's Global Risk Management Operations.	1	**lead**
I'm not sure what I'm going to do, but I'll probably be **heading up** to New York next year.	2	**go to a place**

EXERCISES

A. Complete the sentences with a suitable form of *head up* (e.g., *is heading up*) and one of the words from the box. Be sure to use the correct article (e.g. *a*/*the*) with the noun where required:

export	support	Accounting Oversight Board	recruited	vice-president

1. Rachel Carson will be _____ this project and coordinating with Accounting for _____.
2. Mr. Benson has _____ MDA's _____ division since 1995.
3. I was _____ to _____ the company's glass-container business.
4. Ms. Gibson will become _____, _____ a new strategic planning department.
5. Mary MacDonald has been named to _____ the new _____.

B. Find the error in each sentence:

1. Charlie Nguyen has been told to go to Singapore to heads up MobileNet there.
2. Kathy Cote has been appointed vice-president of worldwide services, headed up ADG's Business Unit.
3. As the new director of engineering, Smith will heading up SimpTech's engineering and new product development strategies.
4. Before heading up PSS, Sullivan worked at Lotus Development Services.
5. Jacobs, who headed up the Ocelot development team, says the package is user-friendly and very powerful.

C. Discussion Question

1. Who heads up the international division of Starbucks? Who heads up marketing at Microsoft?
2. Do some research online to find out, then choose another company and name a person who heads up an important unit, division, or service.

Unit 63: ROLL OUT something

STUDY THESE SENTENCES

The company will use the proceeds of the
sale to **roll out** new products.

1   produce, offer

EXERCISES

A. Rewrite the sentences by replacing the underlined word or phrase with the correct
   form of *roll out* (e.g. *is rolling out*):
   1. GM is planning to <u>release</u> a new van next year.
   2. The clothing chain <u>introduced</u> the Mary-Lou Baker line of women's accessories.
   3. The superstore chain is to <u>utilize</u> its mini-store strategy next year.
   4. When the company <u>showcased</u> its pay-TV decoders, it sold its entire stock in 3
      days.
   5. The US fast food chain <u>opened</u> hundreds of restaurants in China.

B. Complete the sentences with a suitable form of *roll out* (e.g., *is rolling out*) and one
   of the words from the box. Be sure to use the correct article (e.g. *a/the*) with the noun
   where required:

profits	New York show	Europe consumer	personal computers	bank

   1. CCC plans to .... its new consumer line of ....
   2. The CEO said .... will improve when the company .... its new
      breakthrough products.
   3. .... is shutting down branches and .... ATMs in
      supermarkets.
   4. Starsoft .... a set of development tools for Java at ....
   5. Initially, the DigiVision service will be available in the US, but plans are in hand
      to .... the service across .... next year.

C. Discussion Question

   What kind of futuristic product would you be excited to see a car company roll out?
   A software or computer company? A grocery store chain?

Unit 64: DRAW UP something

STUDY THESE SENTENCES

Find an attorney who knows how to **draw up** the kind of contract you need.   **1   create, make, write (up)**

EXERCISES

A. Choose the correct answer(s) to fill in the blanks. There may be more than one correct choice:

1. The consultant helped to .... the turnaround plan.
   (a) drawing up   (b) draw up   (c) drew up
2. We .... a wish list of features and most of these have been included in the new product.
   (a) draw up   (b) are drawing up   (c) drew up
3. Stricter federal security guidelines were .... after the attack.
   (a) drawing up   (b) drawn up   (c) drew up
4. Zencorp .... a list of 2000 potential buyers.
   (a) has drawn up   (b) has drew up   (c) is drawing up
5. Every auto maker .... plans for cars that are more fuel efficient.
   (a) has drawn up   (b) is drawing up   (c) will draw up

B. Complete the sentences with a suitable form of *draw up* (e.g., *is drawing up*) and one of the words from the box. Be sure to use the correct article (e.g. *a/the*) with the noun where required:

loan	companies	package	expenses	executives	agreement

1. I hope you don't mind. I have .... a draft ....
2. They have to .... a business plan before applying for .... from the bank.
3. Shiseido is .... a shopping list of .... to buy.
4. .... are .... plans to expand the company in Asia.
5. The company is .... plans to offer consumers .... of interactive services.
6. The IRS is .... guidelines for entertainment ....

C. Refer back to the sentences in exercise B. What words (nouns) follow draw up? Make a list of the collocations:

draw up   ....
draw up   ....
draw up   ....
draw up   ....

Unit 65: REVIEW
CUT BACK, HEAD UP, ROLL OUT, DRAW UP

A. Choose the correct form of the verb to fill in the blanks:

1. The luxury car maker has .... on advertising this year.
(a) cutting back   (b) cut back   (c) cuts back

2. The packaging company has .... a new business plan that includes cuts in staff numbers.
(a) drawn up   (b) drawing up   (c) drew up

3. Some companies have launched pilot projects that could be .... to most of the country within the next couple of years.
(a) rolling out   (b) rolls out   (c) rolled out

4. Karen Black, who .... the California unit, is now in charge of the national AAT office.
(a) heading up   (b) headed up   (c) head up

5. Philips and its partners will .... a new set-top box for digital broadcasts and web services.
(a) roll out   (b) rolling out   (c) rolled out

6. Industry has .... on money spent for research and development.
(a) cutting back   (b) cut back   (c) cuts back

B. Fill in the blank with the correct form of the correct phrasal verb (cut back (on), head up, roll out or draw up). Use the nouns that collocate with the verbs to help you:

1. The manager .... a list of sales targets for each of the reps.
2. Debt-ridden consumers and companies are .... their spending
3. Ynex intends to offer web-based ads to businesses in the New York region, before .... services to advertisers in other states.
4. Managing Director Steve Nicholson has been appointed to .... KPN's UK division.
5. The hi-tech retailer will .... orders for computers this month.
6. VData Labs .... its X-Act software at a tradeshow in San Francisco last week.

Unit: Human Resources

These phrasal verbs may be used when talking about activities connected with the Human Resources Department (HR). HR deals with hiring and employment issues at a company.

bring in. build up, come in, contract out, cut back, deal with, end up, head up, look for, set up, specialize in, take on

> The company plans to **bring in** someone who **specializes in** accounting to **head up** the finance dept. We are **looking for** a person to **build up** the company's investment arm by **cutting back** costs on **contracting out** non-core services. The person **coming in** will be expected to **set up** a strong management team, **take on** responsibility for strategic planning, and **deal with** issues as they arise.

A. Imagine you are a consultant. What advice would you have for :

1. a company that wishes to expand its website?
2. a boss who needs help managing her schedule?

3. a sales department that has increased orders?
4. a colleague who no longer feels challenged at work?
5. an industry facing a slowdown in the market?

(a) take on an assistant
(b) cut back on excess inventory
(c) look for a new job
(d) contract out to an IT firm
(e) bring in extra staff

B. Circle the word(s) that can be used together with the phrasal verb:

1. **take on** (a) the company (b) a position (c) publicity
2. **set up** (a) an appointment (b) an interview (c) a meeting
3. **end up** (a) ahead (b) money (c) successful
4. **bring in** (a) money (b) investors (c) customers
5. **build up** (a) inventory (b) a reputation (c) a company

C. Answer these questions using full sentences:

1. What do you think it takes for a company to bring in new customers and keep them coming back?

2. What do you specialize in at the company where you work?

3. If you could head up a department or company, what would it be?

4. If you could set up a meeting with any big business mogul, who would it be?

Unit: Advertising and Sales

These phrasal verbs may be used when talking about activities relating to advertising and sales: *come in, come out, cut back, deal with, figure out, focus on, go back, get back, get into, keep up, pick up, roll out, turn out, work on.*

A. Decide which phrasal verbs are connected with:

1. giving attention to something (three answers)
2. reducing or returning to a previous state (three answers)
3. maintaining or increasing something (two answers)
4. producing something (two answers)

B. Read the following paragraph then answer the questions:

I'd like to **set up** a meeting to **work on** a new advertising campaign for ADB. I am delighted to announce that we **came in first** in the competition for this account. We will be **dealing with** Tom Markus, the marketing manager at ADB. Our goal is to **figure out** a marketing strategy that will help the client **pick up** market share in a very competitive environment. ADB wants us to **cut back on** advertising in traditional media and instead **focus on** web advertising in order to **keep up with** the trends of younger buyers. The client is keen to see measurable results, with evidence of sales **picking up** as we **roll out** our campaign.

1. Fill in the blanks with the phrasal verb that best completes these collocations. There may be more than one answer in some cases:

    (a) to _____ a sales/marketing strategy
    (b) to _____ the manager
    (c) to _____ market shares
    (d) to _____ advertising
    (e) to _____ a campaign
    (f) to _____ buying trends

2. Discussion:

    (a) What is the role of a marketing manager? An advertising agency?
    (b) What are the characteristics of a good salesperson?
    (c) Name some current trends associated with younger buyers.
    (d) How do you know when a marketing campaign is successful?

C. Rewrite these sentences by replacing the underlined word(s) with the appropriate phrasal verb. Make any other necessary changes to the sentences.

1. One of the things to emerge from the meeting was the need to launch a new marketing strategy.
2. We're going to return to basics and concentrate on our core energy business.
3. The deals happened to be very profitable.
4. CBF aims to enter the Spanish market.

Unit: Manufacturing

These phrasal verbs may be used when talking about activities connected with the manufacturing process: *build up, comply with, cut back, end up, go through with, keep up with, put in, rely on, roll out, shut down, turn out.*

Agenda: **Questions to consider at the meeting:**

Can we rely on prompt deliveries of materials?
Are we building up too much inventory?
When should we shut down the plant for maintenance?
Are we complying with the new federal regulations on recycling?
Are we doing enough to cut back on power consumption?
Do we have the capacity to keep up with future demand?

A. Match the phrasal verb on the left with its more formal synonym on the right. Use a dictionary, if necessary:

1. build up   close
2. comply with   obey
3. cut back   increase
4. rely on   decrease
5. keep up with   curtail
6. shut down   trust
7. cut back   stay abreast of

B. Which collocation(s) fit with the phrasal verb? Circle all that apply.

1. build up   stock, inventory, a reputation, regulations
2. keep up with   demand, consumption, salary, deliveries
3. rely on   punctuality, consumers, staff, inventory
4. comply with   customers, regulations, orders, products
5. cut back on   demand, workers, the plant, consumption

C. Fill in the blanks with the correct form of one of the following phrasal verbs and one of the nouns from the box. Be sure to add an article (*the/a/an*) where necessary:

VERBS	NOUNS/NPs
go through with	off shore production
build up	chip maker
roll out	factory
turn out	inventory
shut down	GM

1. Workers at .... were .... brand name running shoes.
2. They decided not to .... their plan to purchase ....
3. .... is planning to .... a new van next year.
4. The computer manufacturer may have .... too much .... of memory chips.
5. There is a fear that the hurricane will ....

Unit: Takeovers

The following phrasal verbs may be used when talking about takeovers. A takeover involves one company acquiring or gaining control over another.

come up, draw up, go on, go through, lay off, look at, shut down, take on

> We are **looking at** Allied Farms in terms of the possibility of a merger or takeover. We will get our legal department to **draw up** a contract, but we expect negotiations will **go on** for a while and we cannot be certain that the deal will **go through**. Various difficult issues are likely to **come up** over the next few weeks, including the question of plans to **shut down** some units and **lay off** staff. I am, however, confident that we will **come out** of this period a stronger company, ready to **take on** our competitors in the industry.

A. **Match the phrasal verb on the left with its more formal synonym on the right. Use a dictionary, if necessary:**

1. look at   challenge
2. draw up   emerge
3. come out   continue
4. take on   consider
5. go on   prepare

B. **Create collocations by matching a word from the box with the correct phrasal verb:**

problems   employees   a binding contract   deals   the possibilities   the competition

1. take on ....
2. .... go through
3. lay off ....
4. look at ....
5. .... come up
6. draw up ....

C. **Discussion Questions**

1. Can you think of a company that was recently involved in a takeover bid?
2. Who is usually involved in the negotiations that precede a takeover? Name some of the key players.
3. What are some of the problems that companies may experience after a takeover? What are some of the benefits?
4. Have you known anyone whose job was affected because a company was taken over?

*I believe I'm well-qualified to **head up** the sales division*

*We're **cutting back on** our travel expenses*

Answer key

Unit 1: Deal with
A. 1. 2 2. 3 3. 1
B.
1. The bank deals with a number of US corporations.
2. He likes his job and dealing with people.
3. In my field of work, you deal with a wide variety of issues.
4. Some companies only deal with very wealthy people.
5. The translators have dealt with thousands of pages of documents.
C.
1. We plan to deal with manufacturers in China.
2. There was a recognition that corruption is a problem and that it has to be dealt with.
3. The lawyer said we may have to deal with a lawsuit.
4. The company has to find ways to deal with the drop in sales.
5. All companies now have to deal with environmental concerns.

Unit 2: Look at
A. *Suggested answers*
1. The accountant looked at sales figures for July.
2. He often looks at his computer to check for new email.
3. She recommends looking at utility stocks.
4. We're looking at a variety of ways to cut costs.
5. I always look at a problem and try to solve it step by step.
B.
1. The audit looked at loans made in 2002.
2. The panel will look at both sides of the tax issue.
3. The report looked at smoking trends among teenagers.
4. Look at Asia today. It reinvented its entire economy.
5. The important thing for her is to look at the big picture.
C.
1. I don't know if you've had a chance to look at the book yet.
2. We looked at some potential acquisitions in the UK.
3. Most people look at it as an investment.
4. The study looked at 350 companies.
5. If you look at the average family with two kids, they would pay about $400 in higher taxes.

Unit 3: Set up
A.
1. I hope he's not setting himself up for failure.
2. The state is aiming to set up a job-training program for high school dropouts.
3. Aviana is setting up a low-cost airline called Egg.
4. They contacted the creditors and set up a payment plan.
5. He has already made enough money to set himself up for life.
B.
1. The insurance companies set up mobile offices in Florida.
2. The IT people set up a computer network in the offices.
3. Judy is going to set up a conference call for Wednesday at 10 a.m.

4. The city is setting up a telephone hotline.
5. They contact the creditors and set up a payment plan.
C.
1. The Internet Connection Wizard set up my Internet connection.
2. Please set up a meeting with Larry for Thursday at 9 a.m.
3. Using loans from the SBA, they set up shop in Northern California.
4. The trick is to set up an excellent marketing and distribution system.
5. Rockwell is in the process of setting up a trade center.

Unit 4: Call for
A. 1. 1 2. 3 3. 2 4. 3
B. *Suggested answers*
1. The report called for new restrictions on cigarette advertising.
2. Some shareholders are calling for the resignation of the CEO.
3. The latest order calls for the supply of 5 new aircraft
4. Manufacturers are calling for a reduction in interest rates.
5. The average forecast calls for an overall gain of about 0.3% in retail sales.
6. The new contract calls for a 10% increase in salaries and bonuses.
7. The plan called for a 25% reduction in administrative costs.

Unit 5: Review
A.
1. The CFO is always looking at the bottom line.
2. The harassment incidents were dealt with as they arose.
3. DDK is setting up a 401(k) retirement plan for its employees.
4. The US has called for the deregulation of Japan's insurance industry.
5. The retailer is going to set up an online store.
B.
1. Procedures are in place to deal with charges of discrimination or harassment.
2. I got a call from the guys in Denver. They want to set up a meeting.
3. The study looked at car thefts in metropolitan areas.
4. We are cutting back on the number of suppliers we deal with.
5. We started looking at the idea of taking the company public.
6. My job is to set up a vitamin supply network in the US.
7. The new law calls for tighter controls on the sharing of personal information.
8. Kuwait has abandoned a plan to set up a new oil refinery in Thailand.
9. The burger chain's latest plan calls for 3000 new restaurants world-wide.
10. The unions are calling for a strike against plans to privatize several state companies.

Unit 6: Go on
A. 1. 5 2. 2 3. 4 4. 3 5. 1
B.
1. Currently, there are a lot of mergers going on in the banking world.
2. Last night, the company's spokesperson went on ABC's news program.
3. There is a lively discussion going on between those in favor of the changes and those who oppose the changes.
4. We don't know what was going on in the finance division.
5. I'm sure there will be some more meetings as the week goes on.

Unit 7: Come from

A.
1. The participants come from 17 countries, including Japan, Russia, and Finland.
2. 70% of the world's silk comes from China.
3. The impetus for change comes from the new management team.
4. The gas comes from the Olmos Field in Texas.
5. The savings would come from consolidating 10 offices.

B.
1. The statistics come from the NIH itself.
2. This unemployment figure comes from house-to-house surveys.
3. The winning edge comes from being the first on the block with information.
4. Some new help may come from the World Bank, the biggest single provider of aid.
5. The speaker coming from farthest away will be James Shaw, an entrepreneur from Pennsylvania.

C.
1. No one can imagine where such money will come from.
2. But his greatest challenge could come from the peace process he helped forge.
3. These profits will come from the sale of housing units
4. 70 percent of the increased capital that has been available to Chinese banks since 1988 has come from individual deposits.

Unit 8: Work on

A.
1. The architect is working on a new design for a skyscraper.
2. The pharmaceutical company has been working on drugs to reduce blood pressure.
3. The construction firm is working on a second condominium project.
4. We had been working on them to change their policy.
5. The chairperson was working on the idea that we'd reach an agreement this week.

B. *Suggested answers*
1. Industry researchers have been working on ways of reducing the size of batteries.
2. The company is working on correcting the problem.
3. The biotech company is working on a cancer drug.
4. Last fall, the ad company worked on a pro-smoking campaign for Philip Morris
5. I'm working on the assumption that a meeting will take place very soon.
6. The company said it was working on software improvements.

C. *Students' answers will vary*

Unit 9: Come in

A. 1. 2 2. 1 3. 4 4. 3

B.
1. More than 3000 flights come in and out of New York airports every day.
2. The accounting firm came in for a lot of criticism.
3. If the money doesn't come in, we'll have to take out a loan.
4. A management team came in with a new plan.
5. We are waiting for the checks to come in.

C.
1. The US unemployment rate came in at 6%.
2. The new models are coming in any day now.
3. As the evidence comes in, we can build up a better case.

4. I called and said I would be coming in late today.
5. The Independence Party came in second in elections last fall.
D. *Students' answers will vary*

Unit 10: Review
A.
1. A fax from X came in this morning.
2. The false accounting went on for nearly two years.
3. We're working on a couple of deals right now.
4. Computers will have more power than regular game machines until next winter, when new systems come from Nintendo, Sega and Sony.
5. There are discussions going on with Enron about the use of the money.
B.
1. US consumer data came in on target.
2. The fight has been going on for a number of years.
3. These days many people go on to second careers
4. The computer retailer has been working on a Hispanic marketing strategy
5. The world I come from, everything is economics.
C.
1. After the hurricane, a large number of insurance claims are expected to come in.
2. Hey, what's going on?
3. He is working on a book about globalization.
4. She went on to become one of the richest and most powerful women in the Arab world.
5. He said we should only accept funds that come from federal taxes on products made here.

CorpusLAB 1
1. a. handle b. do business with c. cover
2. go on
3. A. 1 4 6 B. 2 3 C. 5 (Answers my vary)
4. a committee, a meeting
5. come in

Unit 11: Look for
A. *Suggested answers*
1. John is looking for a new business to buy.
2. The phone company is looking for new marketing strategies.
3. A lot of laid-off managers must look for work again.
4. Advertisers are looking for alternatives to TV and radio.
5. Southcorp plans to look for growth in export markets and in Asian ventures.
B.
1. In a new assistant director, the search committee looked for someone who had experience working with service organizations.
2. Factories, palm oil and rubber plantations as well as construction companies, are forced to look for labor outside.
3. If we want to be a player in South East Asia, we must look for possible partnerships in Thailand and Korea.
4. Some buyers say cost isn't the issue when they're looking for quality.
5. Mr. Thomas said he was looking for a new challenge.

Unit 12: Depend on

A. 1. 2 2. 3 3. 1 4. 3 5. 2

B.

1. Depending on the type of hotel, costs range from $50-$250.
2. Success depends on good products at reasonable prices.
3. We've been depending too much on Susan.
4. Many local economies depend on money from visitors.
5. What you make of the new information depends on your perspective.

C.

1. What happens next depends entirely on the government.
2. Many consumers depend on food labels for nutrition information.
3. Italy depends on farming for 3% of its gross domestic product.
4. Mortgage rates vary greatly depending on the product.
5. Our success depends on having a strong sales team.

Unit 13: Pick up

A. 1. 5 2. 1 3. 4 4. 3 5. 2

B.

1. I picked up the phone and called my supervisor.
2. He picked up the tab for the meal.
3. Exports did not pick up because of the high dollar.
4. The online gambling industry is picking up steam.
5. After a bankruptcy someone has to pick up the pieces.

Unit 14: Meet with

A. 1. 2 2. 1 3. 1 4. 2 5. 2

B.

X	form of *meet with*	Y	negative connotation?
marketing campaign	has met with	limited success	yes
new policies	will meet with	public approval	
company's proposal	met with	harsh criticism	yes
attempts to...	met with	vigorous opposition	yes
proposed bills	met with	skepticism	yes
claims	were met with	utter disbelief	yes
talk of the merger	was met with	cautious optimism	somewhat positive

Unit 15: Review

A.

1. The fund is looking for companies that have high growth potential.
2. If possible, I would like to meet with you and discuss my plans for the future.
3. He is able to pick up the phone and make a call to the CEO.
4. The just-in-time approach depends on the components arriving on time.

B.

1. The company picked up the tab for a 3-day retreat in Colorado.
2. Profits will be good if the property market picks up.
3. Local TV stations depend on news programming for a large portion of their revenue.
4. We're always looking for ways to make our products better.
5. I'm gonna meet with the accounting people today.

C.
1. The government may pick up some of the health costs of early retirees.
2. Demand for gasoline has picked up sharply in the last month.
3. Luckily, sales picked up later in the season.
4. If you pick up any magazine, you see a variety of diet ads.
D. 1. yes 2. yes 3. yes 4. yes 5. no

Unit 16: Make up
A.
1. Oil makes up 25% of Venezuela's gross domestic product.
2. We don't know how much money we lost because the numbers were made up.
3. I made up my mind to learn something about computers.
4. The phone company will make up for lost income by charging higher rates.
5. He invested less than $100 to advertise in a local paper and made up some fliers.
B.
1. Many voters made up their mind a long time ago.
2. I'll make up some packets for the conference attendees.
3. Boeing told NASA that it could make up for lost time on the space project.
4. The partner made up a story that I was stealing from the firm.
5. Solar power makes up 10% of the country's supply.

Unit 17: Do with
A.
1. The high price of oil has little to do with the drop in share prices.
2. The cost-cutting has nothing to do with the safety of the airline.
3. Mr. Stewart said he has nothing to do with his wife's finances.
4. Pride may have a lot to do with it.
5. I have a question. It has to do with the overall goal of the report.
B.
1. Most banks don't want anything to do with the credit card company.
2. I had nothing to do with the PPM deal.
3. I know he didn't have anything to do with it.
4. The dispute has nothing to do with us.
5. RTL TV said the change had nothing to do with complaints.

Unit 18: Account for
A. 1. 1 2. 3 3. 3 4. 1 5. 2
B.
1. Sugar accounts for one third of Fiji's exports.
2. Windmills account for about 3500 megawatts of electricity in the US.
3. Deutsche Telekom accounts for about 96 percent of telephone sales in Germany.
4. Memory chips accounted for more than 60% of the company's profit in 2002.
5. The reports did not account for the connection between the cases.

Unit 19: Rely on
A.
1. Housing authorities rely on rental income to meet their operating and maintenance expenses.
2. Retailers these days don't rely solely on conventional marketing techniques.

3. Nintendo's Ultra 64 will still rely on cartridge games while the Sony PlayStation will play compact disc-based games.
4. The company's strategy is to rely on acquisitions to achieve double-digit growth.
5. I relied on the advice of financial professionals.
B.
1. The Korean market is small and so electronics companies rely on exports.
2. For many years auto companies have relied on cash rebates to attract customers.
3. We can't rely on other companies to do our research and development for us.
4. Brazil relies on gas for only 3% of its fuel needs.
5. The company should be able to rely on digital cameras, its traditional cash cow.

Unit 20: Review
A.
1. Technology stocks make up a considerable portion of the NASDAQ index.
2. If exports can't account for the rise in profits, what is the motivating factor?
3. The judge dismissed a portion of the case in which Virgin Atlantic relied on state laws.
4. ``I believe I can do it, and believing in yourself has a lot to do with it."
B.
1. It is estimated that packaging costs account for about half the total cost of making soft-drink products.
2. "I still rely on her every day," he said.
3. In the past, the exports relied on the Hong Kong and Macao markets.
4. The reason for the delay has to do with production difficulties.
5. Officials were unable to immediately account for what caused the machine to malfunction.
C. 1. yes 2. yes 3. no 4. yes 5. yes

CorpusLAB 2
1. deal with 2. met with 3. met with 4. do with 5. met with 6. deal with
2. account for
3. A 2 3 B 1 7 C 4 5 6
4. make up
5. REACTIONS: opposition, limited success, surprise, warm applause, a lot of opposition, little enthusiasm
   PEOPLE: hosptal officials, investment bankers, employees, you, Mr. Belden, your client
6. look for

Unit 21: Take over
A. 1. 2 2. 2 3. 1 4. 2 5. 1
B.
1. Rupert Morley has run the company well since he took over in 2002.
2. San Diego's HomeFed bank was taken over by regulators in 1992.
3. VCS Bank denied Dutch press reports that it plans to take over Credit Lyonnais Bank.
4. Under the reorganization some areas will be increasingly taken over by representatives working in the field.
5. The management firm will take over day-to-day operations from the founder and CEO.
C. Student answers will vary.

Unit 22: Point out
A.
1. She points out that IPOs nearly doubled in 2003.

2. Company officials point out they have hired 18,500 new workers over the last four years.
3. Some analysts point out that the year-over-year gains are not so impressive, considering last year's low earning.
B.
1. The company points out it didn't start the strike, which affected workers in three states.
2. Industry experts point out that the car company has far to go to catch with industry standards for efficiency.
3. I would just point out that I see an adjustment to house prices as the most significant risk here.
4. Mr. Rivlin pointed out that deficit naturally rises during times of economic slack
5. A: It's 12.05.
   B: Thank you Robert for pointing that out (to us).

Unit 23: Give up
A.
1. He gave up his academic career to focus on finance.
2. We had no choice but to keep going. We couldn't give up.
3. If we borrow more money we will be giving up equity in the company.
4. I love farming; I wouldn't give it up for anything.
5. You should never give up hope.
B.
1. He gave up a career in politics to spend more time with his family.
2. He gave up photography to join the army.
3. She gave up a lot of her free time to help new immigrants.
4. Millions of Americans have given up cigarettes.
5. The dollar gave up yesterday's gains against the euro.

Unit 24: End up
A.
1. Some regions such as California could end up not having enough supplies of electric power.
2. The company may end up issuing stock to repay borrowed money.
3. I understand that we could end up collecting less than 100%of what we are owed.
4. If we don't win another large contract, we could end up unemployed.
5. The strike will end up costing the company around $300 million.
B.
1. The company ended up settling the charges by paying a small fine.
2. If we're not careful, we'll end up in debt.
3. He moved to Manhattan and finally ended up working in Los Angeles.
4. The city government may end up with a surplus of unspent money.
5. The entire scheme may end up costing as much as $20 billion.

Unit 25: Review
A.
1. Greg Wolf took over as chief operating officer from Mr. Tyson.
2. On Tuesday, the stock market ended up closing 6.26 percent lower.
3. The Lloyds' agents never gave up their right to sue in U.S. courts.
4. If you don't correct the mistakes now, you're going to end up having to correct them in six months to a year.
5. The analyst points out that the companies price-to-earnings ratio is about 10% higher than its expected growth rate.

B.
1. A veteran Japanese diplomat has taken over as executive director.
2. The market ended up pretty much where it started the year.
3. If you withdraw money from a retirement plan, you give up future tax-exempt growth.
4. The Saatchi firm pointed out the restrictions in the contracts.
5. It is a David and Goliath battle, but we are not going to give up.

Unit 26: Spin off
A.
1. Bally Entertainment spun off Bally Total Fitness in 1999.
2. Highway Express was spun off from Transport Services Inc.
3. The chairman refused to discuss whether the company will spin off any of its new holdings.
4. Payton is being spun off by Quality Department Stores Co.
5. Viacom is unlikely to spin off Blockbuster any time soon.
B.
1. K-C plans to spin off its cigarette-paper and tobacco operations.
2. Sprint is going to spin off its cellular operations.
3. The company will spin off its banking operations to shareholders.
4. The hotel chain announced that it plans to spin off its casino holdings.
5. Ford might spin off its auto-finance unit.

Unit 27: Enter into
A.
1. The corporation has entered into an agreement with YBG for the sale of the manufacturing unit.
2. EGM entered into a five-year marketing services agreement with the AC Group.
3. The company wants to enter into long term strategic arrangements within the Western region.
B.
1. TR Corp has entered into <u>an oil and gas exploration agreement</u> with LDN Gas Corp.
2. SPIC has entered into <u>a strategic alliance</u> with EGM to jointly promote various financial products.
3. The Canadian subsidiary said it has entered into <u>negotiations</u> with Gem World.
4. The company has entered into <u>tentative deals</u> to build two new office blocks.
5. Gas Corp. has entered into <u>financial contracts</u>, allowing it to sell natural gas at set prices.
6. The US companies often enter into <u>partnerships</u> with Chinese or Hong Kong counterparts.
7. The sales data are entered into <u>the computer</u> every day.
8. Sign up and you will be entered into <u>a drawing</u> for concert tickets.

<u>Patterns:</u>
Enter into an agreement
Enter into an alliance
Enter into negotiations
Enter into a deal
Enter into a contract
Enter into a partnership
(Be) entered into a computer
(Be) entered into a drawing

Unit 28: Come up

A.
1. 2 (a) take place in the future
2. 2 (a) be promoted
3. 1 (a)
4. 2 (b)
5. 3
6. 2 (a) appear

B.
1. We came up with the chocolate theme for the ad.
2. A. Are we in on this?
   B. Yeah, your name comes up.
3. *You gotta give me another week to come up with $1000.*
4. Our employees came up with the best selling product.
5. There's a couple of bond deals coming up.

C.
1. That's great that your brother's wedding is coming up.
2. You're going to have problems and it is worthwhile to deal with them as they come up.
3. We came up with the magazine to target Hispanics who were born in the US.
4. A. What about the finance problem?
   B. If it comes up, just say that we're working on it.
5. Let me come up with a plan and I'll get back with you early next week.

Unit 29 Build up

A.
1. The computer manufacturer may have built up too much inventory of memory chips.
2. We have built up our internet operations over the last two years.
3. He acquired the company in 1990 and built it up over the following decade.
4. American Airlines have been trying to build up their business in Asia.
5. MTG has hired a consultant to build up its Canadian operations.

B.
1. Investors are building up their holdings of foreign stocks.
2. A backlog of orders has built up for the popular game machine.
3. The supermarket is gradually building up a loyal customer base.
4. Companies reduced their inventories in May after building them up in April.
5. The automaker sells its latest car at a loss to build up market share.

C. *Students' answers will vary.*

Unit 30: Review

A.
1. The bank has failed to come up with a solution to the loan dispute with ACG.
2. Because of the fall in earning, plans to spin off units have been postponed.
3. The partnerships entered into complex financing and hedging arrangements with Neron.
4. Let me come up with a plan and get back to you next week.
5. RWE has built up a derivatives trading team.

B.
1. We need to come up with a new set of numbers based on projected expenditures.
2. *You gotta give me another week to come up with the $500.*
3. It will take a couple of years to build up our marketing operations.

4. The company will use the capital to build up its sales force.
5. If you try to come up here, you will not be allowed in the building.
C.
1. The board is meeting to decide whether to sell the cable unit or instead spin it off as an independent company.
2. The company may have to come up with more money to honor a collateral call on a $600 million note.
3. EMG has entered into a five-year marketing services agreement with ACG.
4. Neron has entered into an agreement with Warburg for the sale of Netcom.
5. The management will not enter into a transaction that might threaten the company's stability.

CorpusLAB 3
1. 1. build up 2. came up 3. set up 4. end up 5. gave up 6. build up 7. make/made up 8. give up 9. come up 10. make up 11. set up 12. end up
2. point out
3. 1. meeting 2. time 3. money/cash 4. plan/way 5. debt 6. issue/question
4. A 5 6 B 2 C 1 D 3 7
5. an agreement, (agreements) a transaction, (transactions)

Unit 31: Shut down
A.
1. Unemployment will rise when inefficient industries are shut down.
2. Financial markers will shut down for two days this week due to public holidays.
3. The plant was shut down when a leak in a pipe was discovered.
4. The strike shut down one assembly plant in Michigan.
5. She shut down her computer when the meeting started.
B.
1. The refinery was shut down after a leak was detected.
2. Araco Inc. has decided to shut down its zinc mine in Colorado.
3. The investment-management unit was shut down last week.
4. Wall Corp plans to shut down a metal-can production facility in Ohio.
5. The strike shut down car and truck assembly lines.
C.
Students' answers will vary.

Unit 32: Specialize in
A.
1. ATS, which has offices in seven states, specializes in providing temporary office staff.
2. Joel Scott is a turnaround expert who specializes in restructuring large companies.
3. Apple Computer plans several initiatives aimed at promoting sales by resellers who specialize in Apple products.
4. Mr. Steinberger is a management consult at BHW where he specializes in book publishing projects.
5. Georgia Properties is a real estate investment trust, specializing in south-east apartments.
B.
Students' answers will vary.

Unit 33: Find out

A.
1. My boss found that out when he visited Iceland.
2. When I find out what the deal is, I'll let you know.
3. Companies found out that they could cut costs by hiring temporary workers.
4. I found out the hard way that stocks can go down as well as up.
5. Did you take the time to find out if they had insurance?

B.
Students' answers will vary.

C.
Students' answers will vary.

Unit 34: Put in

A. 1. 2 2. 1 3. 3 4. 6 5. 5

B.
1. *Think of what you could do if you put in a little effort.*
2. Part of the new welfare-to-work program was put in place last year.
3. Buyers tend to put in their orders at the end of the month.
4. Carole Jay has been put in charge of West Coast Operations.
5. He puts in fewer than 100 hours a month at the office.

C.
Students' answers will vary.

Unit 35: Review

A.
1. The bug causes the computer to freeze or shut down.
2. W&L is a New York ad agency that specializes in marketing to kids and families.
3. As soon as we found out about the defect, we ordered a recall of the autos.
4. The executives put in a place a new growth strategy.
5. I found out the hard way that stocks can go down as well as up.

B.
1. PTG are taking steps to shut down Inter-TV, an interactive-television venture.
2. Investigators are trying to find out whether company officials destroyed documents.
3. In 1995, the copper-mining operation shut down, taking many businesses with it.
4. RubberCo has put in place a plan to add 30 new employees in entry-level management positions.
5. GM has put Ford in a difficult position.

C.
1. A Texas attorney who specializes in the Freedom of Information Act released a series of confidential IRS memos.
2. The furnace was shut down for two days for annual maintenance.
3. Grear is a partner at S&G, a firm specializing in patent law.
4. The company was forced to shut down its music-sharing website.
5. Find out if other franchisees are making money.

Unit 36: Take on

A. 1. 4 2. 1 3. 2 4. 3 5. 4

B.
1. Ed Cox has taken on an executive role at the firm.
2. We are so busy that we cannot take on any more work right now.

3. When Stevens took on the project he didn't know how hard it would be.
4. The company went bankrupt after taking on too much debt.
5. Taking on too much risk is a common problem for investors.
C.
1. The author taken on by Knopf, a major American publisher.
2. The animal rights campaigner taken on some of the biggest US firms.
3. Netscape tried to take on Microsoft with its web-browser.
4. As managers take on more and more responsibilities, they have less time to encourage and inspire their subordinates.

Unit 37: File for
A.
1. She filed for a tax refund for the year 2005.
2. We plan to file a patent for the new device.
3. The drug company filed for FDA approval for its anti-wrinkle cream.
4. The airline filed for reorganization under Chapter 11 last March.
5. Ten years ago, he filed for personal bankruptcy.
B.
File for a tax refund
File a patent
File for FDA approval
File for reorganization
File for (personal) bankruptcy
C. *Students' answers will vary.*

Unit 38: Put on
A. 1. 5 2. 1 3. 2 4. 4
B.
1. Plans to start the new project will be put on hold until the New Year.
2. The government is putting pressure on the university system to increase enrollments.
3. Italians put about $700 million on their credit cards each year.
4. *Can you put the sales meeting on your schedule?*
5. A local law puts limits on rents for poor people.
C.
The HR manager put him on the short list for the job.
We can put you on the waiting list for the flight.
We don't want customers to be put on hold for more than 2 minutes.
The company was put on the market at $12 million.
The product put millions on the company's bottom line.
D. *Students' answers will vary.*

Unit 39: Go through
A. 1. 3 2. 5 3. 4 4. 1 5. 2
B. Suggested answers
1. a divorce, a mid life crisis, tough times, a process, a job change
2. prices, inflation, ratings, stocks, shares, sales
3. papers, email, tax returns, job applications, bills
4. a lawsuit, a plan, an adoption, a merger, a career change
C.
1. Many companies have gone through a tough period and come out stronger.

2. The government raised interest rates to stop inflation from going through the roof.
3. The management will be looking at cost cutting once the merger goes through.
4. CAG's deal with Holden went through a year ago.
5. We went through three attorneys on this case before we finally settled it.
D. Students' answers will vary.

Unit 40: Review
A.
1. The company decided not to take on the trade union over pensions and other benefits.
2. The Advanced Medical Systems unit has been put on sale.
3. The designer house was put on the market at $2 million.
4. I'd say the odds of the deal going through are 50:50.
5. Spectra filed for Chapter 11 bankruptcy protection last June.
B.
1. *Do you want to go through the list?*
2. You don't know what I am going through at work. It's very stressful.
3. *I have been away and now I am going through my email*
4. There are rumors that the mortgage lender may file for bankruptcy.
5. Let me go through what we have done up to this point.
6. The organization is going through a difficult time.
7. Chairman Bill Mortimer has taken on the additional title of CEO.
8. Generic drugs have to go through an approval process before they can be put on the market
9. The company is determined to go through with the ROC merger.
10. *Is there a process I can go through to help me decided whether to go or stay?*
C.
1. After 20 minutes on hold, I finally got through to customer service.
2. Houston went through boom and bust in the 80s.
3. I wish you would put bagels on the menu.
4. We are gearing up to take on more business.
5. DCI has filed for Chapter 11 to limit its exposure to legal suits.

CorpusLAB 4
1. 1. worked on 2. go on 3. taken on 4. rely on 5. put on 6. rely on 7. take on 8. put on 9. worked on 10. went on
2. go through
3. 1. file for bankruptcy/Chapter 11 2. put in charge 3. put on hold 4. put on the market 5. put in place 6. go through the roof
4. A 2 3 B 1 4 6 C 5 7
5.
1. to be put on hold; was put on the market; has been put on the list
2. Speaking on the phone
3. put the cup on the table

Unit 41: Go into
A. 1. 2 2. 1 3. 4 4. 6 5. 3
B. *Students' answers may vary slightly.*
1. Clare went/is going into journalism.
2. The mine went into production in 1997.
3. The leased planes will go into service next month.

4. Since the early eighties, billions of dollars have gone into research on heart disease.
5. The report on pensions goes/went into great detail on the problems facing many people.

Unit 42: Figure out
A.
1. We owe it to our customers to figure out how we can do a better job.
2. Nobody could figure out where the money was going.
3. It doesn't take a rocket scientist to figure out a solution.
4. We've got to figure out ways to expand the services we provide.
5. We're figuring out how much tax we owe.
B.
1.
I am sure Sandy can figure out why my computer keeps crashing.
I am sure Sandy can figure out that being in charge has its drawbacks.
I am sure Sandy can figure out what the economy will be like next year.
I am sure Sandy can figure out a way to do it.
I am sure Sandy can figure out how to avoid paying state taxes.
2.
I'm trying to figure out why my computer keeps crashing.
I'm trying to figure out what the economy will be like next year.
I'm trying to figure out a way to do it.
I'm trying to figure out how to avoid paying state taxes.
3.
Some companies have figured out what the economy will be like next year.
Some companies have figured out a way to do it.
Some companies have figured out how to avoid paying state taxes.
4.
It didn't take me long to figure out why my computer keeps crashing.
It didn't take me long to figure out what the economy will be like next year.
It didn't take me long to figure out a way to do it.
It didn't take me long to figure out how to avoid paying state taxes.
5.
Everyone is trying to figure out why my computer keeps crashing.
Everyone is trying to figure out what the economy will be like next year.
Everyone is trying to figure out a way to do it.
Everyone is trying to figure out how to avoid paying state taxes.
C. *Students' answers will vary.*
Some suggested answers:

(a) figure out X	(b) figure out what X...
- a solution	- happened
- the bill	- the plan is
- your taxes	- we're facing

Unit 43: Focus on
A.
1. Guy Berne says he plans to focus on acquisitions as way to grow the business.
2. She is focusing on improving inventory control in the warehouse.
3. We can improve results by focusing on inventory management.
4. The retailer decided to focus on quality rather than price.
5. At this company, we focus on results.

B.
1. We're in it for the long haul and we focus on the big picture.
2. The government is now focusing/focused on cutting its debt.
3. Sprint has decided to focus on a series of new wireless products.
4. The company is focusing on long-term brand development.
5. The new executive was brought in to focus on day-to-day operations.
C. *Students' answers will vary.*

Unit 44: Get out
A. 1. 4 2. 1 3. 2 4. 5 5. 3
B.
1. The board wants to get results out faster.
2. He started a business a year after getting out of college.
3. We felt it was time to get out of manufacturing and focus on services.
4. I called you as soon as I got out of my meeting.
5. We have to get the impurities out of the water.
C. *Students' answers will vary.*
Some suggested answers:
1. A person should not continue doing something if s/he cannot handle the stress or pressure. The implication being, if you cannot cope, you should leave the job to someone who can.
2. He needs to be more realistic, stop dreaming. The implication is that he will not be taken seriously by his co-workers.
3. You want the outcome of the meeting to be good, beneficial to the task at hand, the company, etc.

Unit 45: Review
A.
1. Ms. Stern believes the US economy is going into a recession now, but could pull out of it by the end of the year.
2. People have trouble figuring out their tax bill.
3. When the new law goes into effect, smoking will be banned in restaurants.
4. BDG is getting out of the electronics business.
5. Instead of being in the office all day, he wants to get out and meet clients.
B.
1. A new GM car has been designed and will go into production in two years.
2. He managed to figure out how the technology could help his business.
3. Bill quit the university to go into the family business.
4. The new guidelines will not go into effect until next year.
5. ABC Worldwide has gone into partnership with ICL plc.
C.
1. We may go into a recession with these kinds of loan problems.
2. *After 15 years, I wanted to get out of sales.*
3. The executive team is focused on the company's core business.
4. About $400 million of debt could go into default
5. We went into this business because of the high growth potential.
6. Connie Chung, the TV announcer, says she plans to go into business with her husband.
7. Wayne Curtis was a machine technician for 10 years before going into management.
8. The auto manufacturer hasn't yet figured out how to avoid a multibillion dollar tax bill.
9. Lisa went through a number of jobs before going into real estate.

10. Since leaving college, he has been focused on starting his own business.

Unit 46 Get into
A. 1. 2 2. 5 3. 1 4. 3 5. 4
B.
1. There was a report today saying that inspectors are getting into North Korea as early as January.
2. The insurance company got into trouble in the late 80s and early 90s.
3. An estimated half-billion gallons of oil are getting into American waterways every year.
4. All the major studios are getting into the interactive-game business.
5. She was really hoping to get into the MBA program.

Unit 47: Turn out
A.
1. The plant is turning out 1 million DVD players a year.
2. All of the reps turned out for the monthly sales meeting.
3. Last year turned out to be a good one for bondholders.
4. November turned out to be the worst month for retail sales.
5. Workers at the factory were turning out brand name running shoes.
B.
1. It seemed like a good idea at the time, but it turned out not to be.
2. Racket manufacturers turn out new models virtually every year.
3. The photos for the new ad campaign turned out well.
4. She said that oil stocks would rise and it turned out that she was right.
5. August turned out to be a very strong month for exports.
C.
1. The company did well, but not for long, as it turned out.
2. It turns out that most millionaires didn't inherit their money; they made it themselves.
3. The online bookstore isn't turning out any profits yet.
4. The start-up's financing could turn out to be inadequate.
5. Managed care has turned out to be beneficial for drug companies.

Unit 48: Go back
A. 1. 2 2. 3 3. 4 4. 1 5. 3
B.
1. *Do you ever think of going back into sales?*
2. They have gone back on their promise not to compete with us.
3. Some farmers are going back to traditional farming methods.
4. Steve is going back to what he does best: running an airline.
5. We can always go back to the bank and ask for more money.
C.
1. After the accident, we had every factory go back and review their safety procedures.
2. I'd better go back to the office.
3. Now is the time to go back into technology stocks.
4. Once the crisis is over, we can go back to business as usual.
5. We can always go back to the bank and ask for more money.
D. *Students' answers will vary.*

Unit 49: Comply with

A.
1. Sykes said that GHF did not comply with the terms of the contract.
2. I have to go to a workshop on complying with anti-discrimination laws.
3. The spokeswoman said that the company will comply with all consumer protection laws.
4. Mr. Rico said that the bank had complied with all requirements under Swiss law.
5. The company admitted it had not been complying with the conditions of the loan.
B.
1. The energy company has to release its internal (Adj.) emails to comply with the court order.
2. The CEO was accused of not taking reasonable steps (N) to ensure that employees comply with the law.
3. The US has made some progress (N) in complying with the agreement.
4. Drug companies can advertise (V) their products as long as they comply with FDA regulations.
5. Failure to comply with these regulations can result in disciplinary (Adj.) action.

Unit 50: Review

A.
1. I didn't know what I was getting into.
2. *Would you advise going back to school – for other small business owners?*
3. I applied to four universities and got into all of them.
4. The suspicious package found in the mall turned out to be a toaster.
5. We're doing our best to comply with what the committee is asking for.
6. The root causes of the problem go back to the 80s.
7. I've always wanted to get into real estate.
8. *We hope the sale turns out well.*
9. *I know Heidi is not thrilled about going back to Dallas.*
10. *Banking turned out to be not quite what I expected.*
B.
1. yes
2. yes
3. yes
4. yes
5. no

CorpusLAB 5

1. 1. turned out 2. find out 3. found out 4 point out 5. get out 6. get out 7. figured out (found out) 8. turning out 9. figure out (find out) 10. pointed out
2. get into
3. A 1 3 5 7 B 6 C 2 4
4. 1   went into this business
      go into the family business
      go into the office
      go into the stairwell
   2.   go into effect
   3.   go into business
      go into real estate
      go into partnership
      went into liquidation

went into foreclosure

Unit 51: Keep up
A.
1. My gym membership was too expensive to keep up.
2. The state needs the sales tax to keep revenue up.
3. He's spending too much. If he keeps it up, he'll soon be broke.
4. It is a daily battle for the Mom and Pop stores to keep up with the large chains.
5. *Do you keep up with any of your old colleagues?*
B.
1. Their income is not keeping up with the cost of living.
2. If we can keep up the pace, revenues could double in the next three years.
3. It's a constant struggle to keep up with the changing regulations.
4. *We had to increase capacity to keep up with retail demand.*
5. *Keep me up to date on your progress.*

Unit 52: Get back

A.

get back/return to a place
He will return from vacation and get back to work.
He wanted to get back to the office as soon as possible.

get something/someone back again
Bmart said its challenge would be in getting customers back.
Please get any comments back to me by tomorrow.

get back/return to an abstract place/activity
Let's get back to business.
When did you get back from vacation?

get back/return to a previous state, usually for the better
The company needs to get back on the path to healthy growth.
It's good to see your career is getting back on track.

B.
1. We sent him numerous letters, but he never got back to us.
2. The important thing is to get the company back to profitability.
3. I will raise that concern with her and make sure she gets back to you.
4. Please get any comments back to me by tomorrow.
5. He's been out sick and only got back in the office today.
C.
1. *If you could get back to me as soon as you can, I'd really appreciate it.*
2. When Heather gets back, she'll be able to get the information.
3. He was anxious to get back to the hair care business once again.
4. *I'll get back to you with a plan on how to do this.*
5. The goal is to get back to 20% gross profit margins.

Unit 53: Contract out

A.
1. Banks are increasingly contracting IT services out to specialists.
2. Outsourcing involves contracting out to companies those services that are not essential to the core business.
3. The trend among manufacturers is to contract out for legal work, cleaning services and catering.
4. American Motors plans to contract out more non-assembly tasks.

B.
1. Manufacturing of the products is contracted out to keep capital and inventory costs
2. Last May, VVX contracted the job out to Teasewell Services.
3. Airlines may contract out services currently provided in-house, such as maintenance and ticket sales.
4. Communications technology allows companies to contract out most support functions while maintaining the core business in-house.

C. *Students' answers will vary.*

Unit 54: Come out

A. 1. 2 2. 6 3. 4 4. 3 5. 1

B.
1. The story came out that the CEO had threatened to resign.
2. The ex-CEO of the company had to come out of retirement.
3. We were surprised by the sales reports that came out today.
4. The chairman of the board came out squarely against the plan.
5. A new release of the software will come out in July.

C. Students' answers will vary. Some suggested answers:
(a) come out of a slump, bankruptcy
(b) come out with a new initiative, a plan
(c) the truth came out, the secret came out, the product came out

D. *Students' answers will vary.*

Unit 55: Review

A.
1. It came out that the politician had received money from the oil company.
2. The company is trying to remedy the downside of contracting the work out.
3. *I look forward to getting back there to watch a UT game with you.*
4. *Thanks for getting back to me.*
5. I try to keep up with the new technology.

B.
1. The shares fell as more information came out about the company's debt problem.
2. *I'll start on this when I get back.*
3. *We have not come out with an alternative schedule yet.*
4. The truth will come out in the end.
5. To stay profitable, we have to keep up with consumer demands.

C.
1. no
2. yes
3. no
4. yes
5. no

Unit 56: Bring in
A. 1. 3 2. 1 3. 2
B.
1. In order to grow her company, Ms. Clements decided to bring in outside investors.
2. Last quarter, the chairman bought in a well-known cost-cutter to improve the bank's financial controls.
3. The successful promotion brought in a flood of new customers.
4. The company aims to bring in half its revenue from outside the US.
5. The new CEO is probably going to bring in new people.
C. *Students' answers will vary.*

Unit 57: Pay off
A. 1. 3 2. 2 3. 1
B.
1. Using aluminum is costlier, but it pays off because it is easier to install and costs less to maintain.
2. Many consumers are finding it difficult to pay off their credit card debts.
3. Sales are increasing, indicating that the investment in new technology is starting to pay off.
4. The start-up company will put aside some money to pay off investors.
5. The company's global growth strategy is paying off, with strong worldwide sales of light trucks making up for weaker demand in the US.
C. *Students' answers will vary.*

Unit 58: Lay off
A.
1. Factories are shutting production lines and laying off workers because of reduced demand for their products.
2. Carla Smith was laid off last December, but got a new job 3 months later.
3. Lenoco had to lay off 105 of its workforce last year.
4. As part of a restructuring package, the company laid off/is laying off 25% of its workforce.
5. The company says it plans to lay off 2,500 people at a cost of $200 million.
B.
1. The fashion chain closed eight stores and laid off 300 employees.
2. Since being laid off, she has worked in a series of temporary jobs.
3. As phone companies merge, they may lay off more operators and replace them with automated software systems.
4. The company owner had some problems with cash flow, forcing her to lay off three people last year.
5. We want to avoid downsizing and laying people off.
C. *Students' answers will vary.*

Unit 59: Bring out
A
1. Waiters brought out the champagne.
2. Sales are a good way to bring out the crowds.
3. Long flights in overcrowded planes bring out the worst in people.
4. A good boss knows how to bring out the best in people.
5. The auction should bring out the bargain hunters.

B.
1. Intel plans to bring out a new chip next year.
2. You can't wait for someone to bring you out of poverty.
3. Many publishers have brought out encyclopedias on CDROM.
4. We reached a settlement to bring the company out of bankruptcy.
5. ADG is far behind its competitors in bringing out new products.
C. *Students' answers will vary.*

Unit 60: Review
A.
1. The new Madonna album brought in $25 million in its first week.
2. The auto maker has often been slow in bringing out new models.
3. They cut down on spending and started to pay off their debts.
4. The CIO brought in Maldonado to install an automated sales tracking system.
5. After being laid off from three companies, he decided to become an entrepreneur and set up his own company.
6. It is not clear whether a long-term strategy based on aggressive growth will pay off.
B.
1. *I've got all the paperwork at home, I'll bring it in tomorrow.*
2. Prodigal is laying off 250 workers and hiring an outside company to take over its customer service operations.
3. The new CEO is probably going to bring in new people/going to be bringing in new people.
4. We had delays bringing products out last year, but we are moving ahead now.
5. The takeover will give a boost to the PR company and bring in several blue-chip clients.
6. These days traveling by air seems to bring out the worst in people.

CorpusLAB 6
1. 1. up 2. in 3. from 4. in 5. out 6. out 7. up 8. up 9. from 10. out
2. 1. on 2. into 3. through 4. on 5. backn 6. into 7. through 8. on 9. into 10. through
3. keep up
4. 1. business 2. top 3. best 4. track 5. workforce/employees
5. A 2 B 1 3 5 C 4 6
6. get back

Unit 61: Cut back
A.
1. Unitel closed one office in Chicago and cut back staff in the New York office.
2. Manufacturers are working hard to cut back excess inventories.
3. The discount airline cut back its flight schedule by 20%.
4. Higher interest rates will cut back consumer spending.
5. The apparel industry continued to cut back on inventories to reduce financing costs.
B.
1. The Air Force cut back/is cutting back/has cut back/will cut back its planned purchase of smart weapons.
2. Memory chip buyers cut back/are cutting back/have cut back/will cut back their orders because of a slowdown in the laptop computer market.
3. Home builders in California cut back sharply on new construction in October.

4. Computer manufacturers are expected to cut back on orders of microprocessors and DVD drives.
5. Less than 40% of respondents say that they cut back/will cut back on driving, even occasionally, for environmental reasons.
C. *Students' answers will vary.*

Unit 62: Head up
A.
1. Rachel Carson will be heading up the project and coordinating with Accounting for support.
2. Mr. Benson has headed up MDA's export division since 1995.
3. I was recruited to head up the company's glass-container business.
4. Ms. Gibson will become a/the/0 vice-president, heading up a new strategic planning department.
5. Mary MacDonald has been named to head up the/a new Accounting Oversight Board.

B.
1. Charlie Nguyen has been told to go to Singapore to head up MobileNet there.
2. Kathy Cote has been appointed vice-president of worldwide services, heading up ADG's Business Unit.
3. As the new director of engineering, Smith will head up/will be heading up SimpTech's engineering and new product development strategies.
4. Before head up PSS, Sullivan worked at Lotus Development Services.
5. Jacobs, headed up the Ocelot development team, says the package is user-friendly and very powerful.
C. *Students' answers will vary.*

Unit 63: Roll out
A.
1. GM is planning to roll out a new van next year.
2. The clothing chain rolled out the Mary-Lou Baker line of women's accessories.
3. The superstore chain is to roll out its mini-store strategy next year.
4. When the company rolled out its pay-TV decoders, it sold its entire stock in 3 days.
5. The US fast food chain rolled out hundreds of restaurants in China.
B.
1. CCC plans to roll out its new consumer line of personal computers.
2. The CEO said profits will improve when the company rolls out its new breakthrough products.
3. The bank is shutting down branches and rolling out ATMs in supermarkets.
4. Starsoft rolled out a set of development tools for Java at the New York show.
5. Initially, the DigiVision service will be available in the US, but plans are in hand to roll out the service across Europe next year.
C. *Students' answers will vary.*

Unit 64: Draw up
A.
1. The consultant helped to draw up the turnaround plan.
2. We drew up/are drawing up a wish list of features and most of these have been included in the new product.
3. Stricter federal security guidelines were drawn up after the attack.
4. Zencorp has drawn up/is drawing up a list of 2000 potential buyers.

5. Every auto maker has drawn up/is drawing up/will draw up plans for cars that are more fuel efficient.

B.
1. I hope you don't mind. I have drawn up a draft agreement.
2. They have to draw up a business plan before applying for a loan from the bank.
3. Shiseido is drawing up a shopping list of companies to buy.
4. Executives are drawing up plans to expand the company in Asia.
5. The company is drawing up plans to offer consumers a package of interactive services.
6. The IRS is drawing up guidelines for entertainment expenses.

C.
Draw up an agreement
Draw up a plan/plans
Draw up a list
Draw up guidelines

Unit 65: Review

A.
1. The luxury car maker has cut back on advertising this year.
2. The packaging company has drawn up a new business plan that includes cuts in staff numbers.
3. Some companies have launched pilot projects that could be rolled out to most of the country within the next couple of years.
4. Karen Black, who headed up the California unit, is now in charge of the national AAT office.
5. Philips and its partners will roll out a new set-top box for digital broadcasts and web services.
6. Industry has cut back on money spent for research and development.

B.
1. The manager drew up a list of sales targets for each of the reps.
2. Debt-ridden consumers and companies are cutting back their spending.
3. Ynex intends to offer web-based ads to businesses in the New York region, before rolling out services to advertisers in other states.
4. Managing Director Steve Nicholson has been appointed to head up KPN's UK division.
5. The hi-tech retailer will cut back on orders for computers this month.
6. VData Labs rolled out its X-Act software at a tradeshow in San Francisco last week.

Unit: Human Resources

A. 1. d 2. a 3. e 4. c 5. b
B. 1. a, (e.g., *take on Microsoft*) b 2. a, b, c 3. a , c 4. a, b, c 5. a, b, c
C. *Students' answers will vary.*

Unit: Advertising and Sales

A. *Suggested answers*
1. deal with, figure out, focus on
2. cut back, go back, get back
3. keep up, pick up
4. roll out, turn out

B.
1.
(a) to figure out a sales and marketing strategy

(b) to deal with the manager
(c) to pick up market shares
(d) to cut back on advertising
(e) to work on/roll out a campaign
(f) to keep up with buying trends
2. *Students' answers will vary.*
C.
1. One of the things to come out of the meeting was the need to turn out a new marketing strategy.
2. We're going to go back to basics and focus on our core energy business.
3. The deals turned out to be very profitable.
4. CBF aims to get into the Spanish market.

Unit: Manufacturing
A.
1. build up   increase
2. comply with   obey
3. cut back   curtail
4. rely on   trust
5. keep up with   stay abreast of
6. shut down   close
7. cut back   decrease
B.
1. build up stock, inventory , a reputation
2. keep up with demand, consumption, deliveries
3. rely on punctuality, consumers, staff
4. comply with regulations, orders
5. cut back on demand, workers, consumption
C.
1. Workers at the factory were turning out brand name running shoes.
2. They decided not to go through with their plan to purchase the chip maker.
3. GM is planning to roll out a new van next year.
4. The computer manufacturer may have built up too much inventory of memory chips.
5. There is a fear that the hurricane will shut down offshore production.

Unit: Takeovers
A.
1. look at   consider
2. draw up   prepare
3. come out   emerge
4. take on   challenge
5. go on   continue
B.
1. take on the competition
2. deals go through
3. lay off employees
4. look at the possibilities
5. problems come up
6. draw up a binding contract

INDEX

give up a career 36
give up gains 36
give up one's free time 36
go back 70, 73, 89, 97
go back to business as usual 71
go back to school 70, 72, 89
go back to square one 70
go back to the drawing board 70
go into 62, 67, 75, 89
go into business 75
go into debt 62
go into detail 62, 75
go into effect 62, 75, 89
go into liquidation 62, 75
go into recession 62
go on 14, 19, 20, 60, 89, 99
go on and on 14
go on sale 89
go on TV 14
go through 57, 59, 60, 89, 99
go through a difficult time 59
go through the roof 57, 60
go through training 58
go through with 57, 98

head up 92, 95, 96

keep up 76, 83, 89, 97
keep up on 76
keep up with 76, 98
keep up with demand 76, 98

lay off 86, 88, 99
lay off workers 86
let go 86
look at 9, 13, 99
look at both sides 9
look at the big picture 9
look for 22, 26, 33, 96
look for a position 26
look for a job 96
look for work 22

make up 27, 31, 32, 45
make up a story 27
make up for lost time 27, 45
make up one's mind 27
meet with 25, 26, 32, 33
meet with approval 25
meet with opposition 25, 33

meet with success 25, 33

nothing to do with 28

pay attention 64
pay off 85, 88
pay off a debt 85
pick up 24, 26, 32, 97
pick up market share 24, 32, 97
pick up speed 26
pick up the phone 24, 26
pick up the pieces 24
pick up the tab 24, 26
point out 35, 38, 45, 74
point out a problem 35
put in 50, 52, 60, 98
put in a bid 51
put in a request 50
put in an order 50
put in charge of 50, 51, 60
put in effort 50, 60
put in place 50, 52, 60
put in time 50, 51
put limits on 55
put on 55, 59, 60, 61
put on hold 55, 56, 60, 61
put on sale 59
put on the market 55, 56, 60
put on the short list 56
put on the waiting list 56
put on the web 55
put pressure on 55, 61
put the brakes on 61

rely on 30, 31, 60, 98
roll out 93, 95, 97, 98
roll out a product 93

set oneself up 10
set up 10, 13, 45, 96
set up a committee 21
set up a meeting 10, 21, 45, 96, 97
set up an appointment 96
set up shop 10, 21, 45
shut down 47, 52, 98, 99
shut down a computer 47
shut down operations 47
something has come up 41
something to do with 28
specialize in 48, 52, 96